D1634232

POCKET

GARDENING
GUIDES

VEGETABLES

❖

DAVID SQUIRE

POCKET

GARDENING
GUIDES

VEGETABLES

❖

DAVID SQUIRE

Illustrated by Vana Haggerty

TIGER BOOKS INTERNATIONAL
LONDON

Designed and conceived by

THE BRIDGEWATER BOOK COMPANY LTD

Art Directed by PETER BRIDGEWATER

Designed by TERRY JEAVONS

Illustrated by VANA HAGGERTY FLS

Edited by MARGOT RICHARDSON

Managing Editor ANNA CLARKSON

CLB 3505

This edition published in 1995 by

TIGER BOOKS INTERNATIONAL PLC, London

© 1995 Colour Library Books Ltd,

Godalming, Surrey

Printed and bound in Singapore

All rights reserved

ISBN 1-85501-488-2

CONTENTS

POCKET GARDENING GUIDES

HISTORY OF VEGETABLES

❖

DURING *the nineteenth century, Esther Copley, a clergyman's wife, was dedicated to improving the diet and conditions of cottagers and the poor. In* The Complete Cottage Cookery *she told how to make the best possible use of vegetables.*

ROWING vegetables is a popular part of gardening. Each year, seed companies offer further exciting varieties, many ideal for sowing in small gardens where every yard is precious. Some of these are ideal for growing in containers on patios; even hanging baskets can be planted with tomatoes, cucumbers and colourful peppers.

In past years, large estates set aside special areas for vegetables, while in cottage gardens informality was a central theme; although they were sometimes grown in formal lines they were often sown or planted among other plants.

On country estates there were a few advocates of closely associating food-growing areas with the rest of the garden. William Cobbett (1763–1835) – a radical reformer who travelled through much of England – when talking about vegetable gardens suggested: 'that it is the most miserable taste to seek to poke away the kitchen-garden, in order to get it out of sight. If well managed, nothing is more beautiful.' And even if houses did not have a garden, the idea of 'allotments' was gaining in popularity. Their size ranged from ten roods (about one-sixteenth of an acre/0.025 hectare) to several acres.

During the Victorian era, many books and magazines featured vegetable gardening, and many seed companies were being started in the USA and Britain.

THE GROTESQUE

'Monstrous broccoli' were illustrated in The Gardeners' Chronical *in 1856 (below). The bizarre and unusual often appealed to the Victorians.*

Cabbages that appear to grow on stilts (above) were grown in Jersey, and in the early part of the 1800s they were featured in The Gardener's Magazine.

THE UNUSUAL

Many unusual vegetables were grown by early Victorians. Skirret, planted for its sweet and white roots, was well known, but soon declined in popularity.

Tree Onions were known in the early 1880s and are still popular today. The bulbs are borne at the top of stems often 60cm/2ft high.

grew more than forty different vegetables, including garlic, globe artichokes and capsicums. Seeds and plants were also available through the many horticultural societies that were being formed.

EXHIBITIONS

Horticultural shows did much during the nineteenth century to capture the attention of vegetable growers. Financial prizes usually ranged from ten to fifteen shillings, while a campaign by William Robinson to encourage the cultivation of asparagus was far more generous. Seed companies were very generous, frequently awarding magnificent cups, but too often they were given to the owner of the garden, not to the gardener himself.

KITCHEN GARDENS

William Cobbett described an average-sized gentleman's kitchen garden during the early years of the nineteenth century as about 60m/200ft long, 40m/132ft wide and enclosed by a 3.6m/12ft wall. There could also be ditches and hedges to keep out children and animals. Such barricades were not possible in cottage gardens. Even at this early time, some gardens

HORTICULTURAL *shows provided the opportunity to make 'growing your own' vegetables more popular.*
Here is an arrangement of fifteen vegetables, illustrated in The Amateur's Kitchen Garden *(1877) by the famous gardening writer James Shirley Hibberd. As well as writing about vegetables, he was well known for his thoughts about garden flowers and bedding schemes.*

TOOLS YOU WILL NEED

❖

STRONG tools that are easy and pleasant to use are essential. Before buying any garden tool, handle it to ensure it can be easily manipulated and is not too large or heavy. Usually, the more you pay for a tool, the better and longer lived it will be. At the top of the range there are stainless-steel tools, but unless these are used frequently, one of lesser quality is quite adequate.

MECHANIZATION

On a garden scale, spades and forks and other hand tools are quite adequate. But for large areas, such as allotments, powered tools with revolving blades make soil cultivation easier and quicker. Often, these can be hired.

MAINTENANCE

The life expectancy of tools very much depends on the way they are used and maintained. Never strain and bend tools, especially spades and forks. After each use, wash, wipe dry and oil bright-metal parts. Wipe plastic handles and coat wooden parts in linseed oil.

TYPES OF HANDLE

There are three types of handle: the T-shaped, D-outline, and D-Y shape. The D-Y is popular, differing from the D-type in that the position where the handle joins the shaft is Y-shaped.

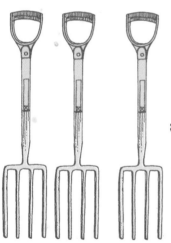

GARDEN FORKS *are often used to dig heavy, wet, clayey soil in winter. Also, they are ideal for breaking down large clods of soil in spring. Like spades, they range in size, with prongs 23cm/9in to 27cm/11in long. Potato forks (right) have wide, slightly blunt-ended tines.*

A STRONG *spade is essential. Digging types have blades about 27cm/11in deep and 19cm/7½in wide. A border type (also known as a lady's spade) is 23cm/9in deep and 14cm/5½in wide. Handle lengths range from 72cm/28in to 82cm/32in long.*

WATERING-CANS *formed of strong plastic or galvanized metal (some are also painted) are essential for watering seedlings, applying liquid feeds and when using weed-killing chemicals. (If at all possible, always use a separate watering can for this purpose.)*

HAND TROWELS *and forks are essential for planting young plants. Choose one with a strong, comfortable handle.*

LARGE DIBBERS *are invaluable for planting young cabbages. Some dibbers have metal tips. Onion hoes enable narrow rows to be weeded.*

GARDEN LINES *are used to form straight rows. Proprietary types are easier to use than two sticks and a ball of twine.*

CLOCHES

Cloches are available in several sizes: tent types have just two panes of glass, while barn ones are higher (suitable for taller crops) and formed of four sheets.

DUTCH HOES *(left), rakes and draw hoes (right) are essential. Choose models that are easy to use and keep clean. Handle lengths vary.*

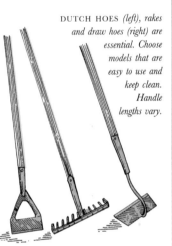

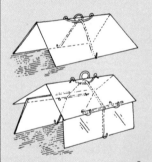

TUNNELS *(plastic or polythene sheeting) are cheaper than glass.*

Cold frame

THREE-PRONGED *cultivators are used to scarify and aerate the soil. Most have handles 1.5–1.8m/ 5–6ft long, but some are short and ideal for infirm gardeners who operate from kneelers. They are operated by pulling, which is usually easier than pushing for elderly people. Some of these cultivators are available with clip-on heads, so that the handle length can be quickly changed. Some also have five-pronged heads.*

RAKES *(above, centre) are essential for levelling soil.*

PREPARING THE SOIL

❖

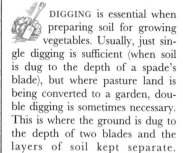

DIGGING is essential when preparing soil for growing vegetables. Usually, just single digging is sufficient (when soil is dug to the depth of a spade's blade), but where pasture land is being converted to a garden, double digging is sometimes necessary. This is where the ground is dug to the depth of two blades and the layers of soil kept separate. Fortunately, double digging is rarely necessary, as it is time consuming and very heavy work.

BENEFITS OF DIGGING

Apart from making the area look tidy, there are other advantages:

• Allows air to penetrate the top 25cm/10in of soil.

• Ensures water drains from the surface, although if the subsoil is waterlogged, water may still rest on the surface during exceptionally wet winters.

• Enables the roots of plants to travel freely through the soil.

• Allows decomposed garden compost and manure to be mixed with the soil.

• Exposes large lumps of soil during winter, enabling the action of frost, wind and rain to break them down. By spring, the soil surface is fine and crumbly.

• Soil pests, such as cockchafer grubs, can be exposed to frosts during winter, thereby helping to reduce their numbers. Leaving grubs on the surface also exposes them to birds, who often wait eagerly to see what each spadeful of soil will reveal.

• Enables annual weeds to be buried. This kills them, but perennial types such as docks and thistles must be removed and burned. If left, they will grow again during the following year. Weeds such as Ground Elder and Horsetail are especially pernicious and every part must be removed to prevent them re-occurring during the following year.

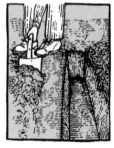

1. SINGLE DIGGING *soil in winter is essential in order to prepare already cultivated ground for sowing or planting crops during the following spring and summer. First, dig a trench (the depth of a spade's blade and about 38cm/15in wide) across one end of the plot.*

2. EVENLY SPREAD *decomposed farmyard manure or garden compost in the trench. Also, skim off annual weeds and invert these into the trench. But dig out and burn all troublesome perennial types. If left, they will appear again during the following year.*

3. WHEN DIGGING, *do not invert excessively large pieces of soil at one time as working this way will inevitably tire you. First, section off a piece of soil about the width of the spade's blade; insert the blade vertically and at a right-angle to the trench.*

4. INSERT *the spade vertically, so that a piece of soil about 10cm/4in thick can be removed. If the soil is heavy, reduce the size; while if light the piece of soil can be slightly larger.*

5. PUSH *the blade right into the soil. It is essential that the soil is dug to an even depth. At this stage, hold the spade by its handle and as close to the blade as can be easily reached.*

6. LIFT *the spade and, with a flick of the blade, turn the soil upside down, so that weeds earlier on the surface are in the base of the trench. Proceed systematically along the row in the same way.*

NO-DIGGING PHILOSOPHY

Many gardeners grow superb vegetables without ever having to dig their soil. Instead, crops are planted on top of compost regularly placed on the soil's surface. Advocates of this method claim that it is a natural way to grow plants. However, it is only practical on light, well-drained and aerated soils which are free from perennial weeds. To many gardeners, the cost and difficulty of buying vast amounts of compost each year is a problem. On most soils, especially clay types, digging over the soil annually usually produces larger and better crops.

COMPOST CONTAINERS

The creation of garden compost from kitchen waste and soft parts of garden plants is essential in the yearly cycle for returning nutrients to the soil and incorporating bulky organic material that aids moisture retention. Proprietary compost bins are available, while others can be constructed from wire-netting or wood. Do not make them more than 1.2m/ 4ft wide.

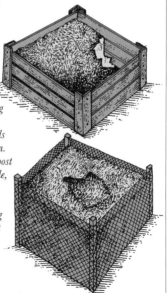

CROP ROTATION

❖

THE same types of vegetables must not be grown continuously on the same piece of soil. If this happens, there is an increase in pests and diseases. Also, the soil becomes depleted of certain plant foods and growth diminishes. However, there are some crops, such as asparagus and rhubarb, which are left in one position for many years but, in general, the best crops are produced when plants are rotated annually. Additionally, do not put seed-beds (where young seedlings are raised) in the same position each year.

	PLOT ONE	PLOT TWO	PLOT THREE
FIRST YEAR	SOIL PREPARATION 1 Beetroot • Carrots Jerusalem artichokes Parsnips Potatoes Salsify Scorzonera	SOIL PREPARATION 3 Aubergines • Beans Capsicums • Celery Celeriac • Leeks Lettuce • Marrows Onions • Peas • Spinach Sweetcorn • Tomatoes	SOIL PREPARATION 2 Broccoli Brussels sprouts Cabbage • Cauliflowers Kale • Kohl Rabi Radishes • Swedes
SECOND YEAR	SOIL PREPARATION 3 Aubergines • Beans Capsicums • Celery Celeriac • Leeks Lettuce • Marrows Onions • Peas • Spinach Sweetcorn • Tomatoes	SOIL PREPARATION 2 Broccoli Brussels sprouts • Cabbage Cauliflowers • Kale Kohl Rabi • Radishes Swedes • Turnips	SOIL PREPARATION 1 Beetroot • Carrots Jerusalem artichokes Parsnips Potatoes Salsify Scorzonera
THIRD YEAR	SOIL PREPARATION 2 Broccoli Brussels sprouts Cabbage Cauliflowers Kale • Kohl Rabi Radishes • Swedes	SOIL PREPARATION 1 Beetroot • Carrots Jerusalem artichokes Parsnips Potatoes Salsify Scorzonera	SOIL PREPARATION 3 Aubergines • Beans Capsicums • Celery Celeriac • Leeks Lettuce • Marrows Onions • Peas • Spinach Sweetcorn • Tomatoes

SOIL PREPARATION 1
When preparing the soil, neither add lime nor dig in manure. Instead, rake in a general fertilizer a couple of weeks before planting or sowing.

SOIL PREPARATION 2
When preparing the soil in early winter, dig in garden compost or manure. Lime the soil in late winter and later rake in a general fertilizer prior to sowing or planting.

SOIL PREPARATION 3
When preparing the soil in early winter, dig in garden compost or manure. If the soil is acid, apply lime in late winter and rake in a general fertilizer prior to sowing or planting.

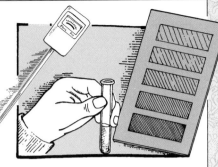

ASSESSING *soil to see if it is acid or alkaline is easy. Most lime-testing kits use chemicals that when mixed with soil produce a colour reaction which can be compared with a colour chart. More recent methods involve the use of a probe which when pushed into soil indicates the pH on a dial, ideal for gardeners who are red–green colourblind.*

THE ROTATION

Vegetables can be arranged into three different types, and it is plants within these groupings that are rotated each year.

• Group one (Root crops): These include beetroot, carrots, Jerusalem artichokes, parsnips, potatoes, salsify and scorzonera.

• Group two (Brassicas): These include broccoli, Brussels sprouts, cabbages, cauliflowers, kale, kohl rabi, radishes, swedes and turnips.

• Group three (Other crops): These include aubergines, beans, capsicums, celery, leeks, lettuce, marrows, onions, peas, spinach, sweetcorn and tomatoes.

Soil preparation for each of these types of crop differs slightly and is indicated in the chart on the opposite page.

CATCH CROPPING

Also known as intercropping, this is when a fast growing and rapidly maturing crop such as radishes is grown between slower growing plants. Examples include spinach between rows of leeks, and lettuces grown between rows of trench celery. The routine of growing catch crops helps to prevent the growth of weeds.

TO MAKE YOUR SOIL MORE ALKALINE

SOIL	HYDRATED LIME	GROUND LIMESTONE
Clay	610g/sq yd (18oz/sq yd)	810g/sq m (24oz/sq yd)
Loam	410g/sq m (12oz/sq yd)	540g/sq m (16oz/sq yd)
Sand	200g/sq m (6oz/sq yd)	270g/sq m (8oz/sq yd)

The lime required to decrease acidity of soil depends on the form in which it is applied and the type of soil. These amounts decrease acidity by about 1.0 pH. Aim for a pH of about 6.5.

RAISING NEW PLANTS

❖

RAISING healthy, strong plants is essential; weak, spindly and unhealthy ones never recover. Many vegetables are raised by sowing seeds where they are to grow and mature; others are sown in seed-beds and transferred later.

In early winter, prepare a seed-bed by digging the soil. Do not break down the surface soil as rain, wind and frost will do this. If late winter and early spring are dry, thoroughly water the area with a sprinkler. When the weather is fine and the soil surface barely dry, prepare it for seed sowing, in the way indicated below.

Sow seeds evenly and thinly, and cover them by either straddling the row and shuffling along, or pulling soil over them with the back of an iron rake. Firm the soil over them and carefully label both ends of the row.

PREPARING A SEED-BED

1. SINGLE DIG *the soil in early winter. In spring, shuffle sideways over the ground to evenly consolidate the soil.*

2. USE *an iron rake to level the surface and to create an evenly deep tilth into which seeds can be sown.*

3. STRETCH *a garden line across the seed-bed and use the sharp point of a stick to create drills 12–18mm/½–¾in deep.*

4. AN ALTERNATIVE *way to form a drill is with the edge of a draw hoe. Take care not to make drills excessively deep.*

1. WHEN *planting, use a dibber or trowel. Push it about 15cm/6in into the ground. Hold the plant by several leaves and dangle its roots in the hole. Use the dibber to lever soil tightly around the roots of young newly-planted plants.*

2. IF PLANTS *are well rooted and have masses of roots, a trowel is better than a dibber. Form a hole large enough to take the roots, then firm soil over them. On light, sandy soils, use the heel of your shoe to ensure the soil is really firm.*

3. AFTER *planting them, thoroughly water the soil to ensure it is in close contact with the roots. Gently trickle water from a watering-can. If the surrounding soil is dry, soak it to prevent plants being immediately robbed of moisture when planted.*

TRANSPLANTING YOUNG PLANTS

If seeds have been sown too thickly it is essential to thin the seedlings as soon as they are large enough to be handled. Ensure soil is re-firmed around their roots, then water them thoroughly but gently. When young plants are large enough to be handled they can be moved to their permanent positions. A couple of days before transplanting them, thoroughly water both the seed-bed and the area into they will be transplanted. If this task is neglected, and the weather is hot and dry, the plants may die.

If possible, choose a cloudy day when transplanting them. When lifting the young plants, use a garden fork to loosen the soil; gently place them in a box lined with moist newspaper or sacking and cover them. Do not dig up more plants than can be planted within thirty minutes, especially if the weather becomes hot. A garden line is essential to ensure that the rows are neat and straight, and use either a dibber or trowel to plant them (see above).

RAISING PLANTS

Vegetables initially raised in a seed-bed include:
- *Asparagus (to form crowns)*
- *Broccoli*
- *Brussels sprouts*
- *Cabbages*
- *Calabrese*
- *Cauliflowers*
- *Kale*
- *Leeks*

Vegetables initially raised in gentle warmth in a greenhouse or garden frame include:
- *Aubergines*
- *Celery*
- *Celeriac*
- *Early onions*
- *Early leeks*
- *Sweetcorn (can also be sown outdoors, directly into its growing position, where the seedlings are subsequently thinned to leave the strongest.)*
- *Sweet Peppers*
- *Tomatoes*

SOWING SEEDS

❖

THE five essential steps of raising plants from seeds when sown in the positions where they are to grow are detailed here. The steps are:

• Forming drills that are uniformly deep and at the correct depth for the seeds. If too deep, the seeds will not germinate, and if shallow the seedlings may not become properly established.

• Sowing seeds evenly and thinly.

There is no advantage in sowing seeds thickly (often just to use up a packet) and, indeed, it is harmful. Additionally, sowing seeds thinly reduces the necessity to thin seedlings too early, before they are established.

• Covering the seeds with an even depth of soil and evenly firming it over them ensures uniform germination. While doing this, try not to spread the

DRILLS *can be formed in several ways. The most usual way is with a corner of a draw hoe. Depths vary, but they are usually 12mm/½in to 18mm/¾in. Always use a garden line to ensure the drill is straight and parallel with neighbouring rows.*

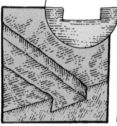

FLAT-BOTTOMED DRILLS *are usually reserved for sowing garden peas. Use a draw hoe to form a trench about 6cm/2½in deep and 23–25cm/9–10in wide. Peas are sown in three rows, with the central row staggered with the others.*

POTATOES *need to be sown in drills about 15cm/6in deep. This is best done by using a garden line and a spade. Ensure the base of the drill is broad, so that the potato tubers sit snugly and firmly in the bottom of the row.*

SOWING SEEDS *so that they do not touch is an art. The normal way for small seeds is to put a few into the hand and to allow them to trickle out very slowly and evenly from between the forefinger and thumb.*

LARGER SEEDS, *such as garden peas and beans, are spaced out along drills: those of broad beans and garden peas are spaced 10–13cm/4–5in apart, while French beans are put 5–7.5cm/2–3in apart.*

SOME SEEDS, *such as sweetcorn, when sown in the open in warm areas, are positioned in groups of three and after germination the weakest plants removed to leave one strong plant at each position.*

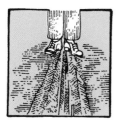

COVERING *drills and evenly firming soil over seeds is essential. A traditional way is to straddle a row and, with feet in a V formation, shuffle along, pushing soil over the seeds.*

THE BACK *of a rake can be used to pull and push friable soil into drills and over seeds. Do not use the prong side, as this may cause the seeds to spread between the rows.*

AFTER *seeds have been evenly covered with soil, firm it with the top of a metal rake. If the surface needs to be raked to make it even, do this shallowly and along the direction of the row.*

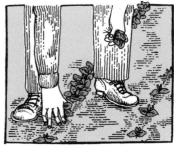

THINNING *seedlings is essential. If left, they become congested and straggly, etiolated and susceptible to diseases. Thinning is normally done in two stages; the first to half the intended spacing and later to the full distance. Place the seedlings that have been*

removed in a box and then on a compost heap. If left on the soil they encourage the presence of pests and the onset of diseases. Ensure that the roots of the remaining seedlings have not been loosened. Re-firm them, and then lightly water the soil.

seeds sideways, as apart from being wasteful it makes early weeding, especially between the rows, very difficult.

• Thinning seedlings is essential to ensure that the plants are strong and healthy. The distances apart vary from crop to crop and these are detailed for the specific vegetables throughout this book. There is no advantage in growing plants too close together, as they become congested, do not mature properly and fail to reach their full size.

• Moisture is the other essential part of germinating seeds and establishing seedlings.

FLUID SOWING

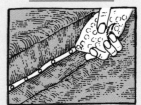

Conserving moisture around seeds is essential while they are germinating. This can be achieved by mixing seeds with wallpaper paste and squeezing the mixture out of a plastic bag into the drill.

LOOKING AFTER PLANTS

❖

 VEGETABLE plants are at their most susceptible to damage when young and not established. Also, at that stage they are tender and likely to be attacked by pests and diseases (see pages 58 and 59).

Keeping the soil free from weeds and watering plants is a major task and one that takes the most time. Regularly hoe between plants, especially after applying powdered fertilizers. If hoeing is neglected there is a chance that the fertilizer will be washed into

contact with young, soft stems and leaves and burn them.

Take great care when using weed-killing chemicals in vegetable plots, as there is a chance that chemicals could drift on the wind and kill plants other than weeds. And before using weed-killers always check with the label. The problem of using weed-killers is increased in small vegetable plots and especially where a wide range of plants are grown; some may be nearly mature, while others are perhaps at their seedling stage.

WATERING *plants is essential, especially when they are young and not fully established. Watering-cans are ideal for watering newly transplanted plants, or young seedlings when they have been recently thinned.*

ROTARY SPRAYERS *enable large areas to be watered. Gentle sprays over a long period are better than a flood of water for a few minutes, which may cause soil erosion or damage to the soil structure.*

OSCILLATING SPRAYERS *are better than rotary ones when watering rectangular areas. Several types are available; avoid those that produce large water droplets, especially if the garden is on a slope.*

WATER TIMERS

Watering vegetable plots and other parts of gardens is far more sophisticated now than it was ten or more years ago. Nowadays, it is possible to use a battery-operated timer which turns water on and off at pre-set times. This enables water to be applied at night when the loss through evaporation is much less than during a hot day. Each timer must be fitted close to the

mains water supply and all joints between it and the tap made secure. If these junctions are weak or ill-fitting they will drip water. And if the tap is left on and with the timer operating throughout a holiday, the area could become excessively wet. Always remember to check with your local water authority to find out if a special licence is required to operate a garden sprinkler.

WEEDS *are a continual problem in vegetable gardens and must be removed before they suffocate young plants. Always dig up and burn perennial weeds; if parts are left in the soil they will continue to grow.*

PULL UP *annual weeds and place on a compost heap. Never leave them on the soil as they encourage the presence of pests and onset of diseases. Watering the soil the previous day makes them easier to pull up.*

REGULARLY *hoe between rows of seedlings and plants to eradicate weeds. Hoeing breaks up crusty soil and allows air and water to enter more freely. Additionally, a fine tilth acts as a mulch and reduces moisture loss.*

ONION HOES *are ideal for hoeing around seedlings and small plants. Pick up annual weeds and place them on a compost heap. Keeping the hoe's blade sharp by using a file makes it much more efficient to use.*

FORMING *a 7.5cm/3in-thick layer of well-decayed garden compost around plants (but not touching) prevents weed growth and keeps the soil moist. Before applying, remove all weeds and water the soil.*

BLACK PLASTIC *is ideal for forming a mulch. Remove weeds and water the soil, then roll out the plastic and insert its edges into small slit-trenches. When planting, make small slits in the plastic.*

DRIBBLE BARS *which fit on spouts of watering-cans are ideal for applying weed-killing chemicals. Keep a watering-can specially for this job and always carefully read instructions for the chemical's use.*

PROTECTION FROM BIRDS

Tunnels formed of wire netting are ideal for protecting seeds and young seedlings from the ravages of birds. Use wire hooks to secure the edges to the ground and place netting over the ends to prevent birds wandering inside the wire hoop, scratching about and totally disturbing the soil and seeds.

ARTICHOKES – GLOBE

❖

ONCE established, Globe Artichokes will continue producing large, scale-like flower-heads for four or five years. Then, it is best to plant further suckers and, after about a year, remove the old plants. The plants grow 1.2–1.5m/4–5ft high.

During the first year, after being planted, a few heads will develop but they seldom mature and are therefore best cut off in autumn. In the second year, each plant will produce about ten flower-heads. Cut them, together with 5–7.5cm/2–3in of stem, when the globes are large and ball-like but before the scales open.

In late summer and early autumn, cut off all immature heads and later, in early winter, cut down plants to just above ground level. To protect the roots in winter, cover them with straw. In spring, remove this covering and dust a general fertilizer around the plants. Lightly hoe and water this into the soil. During summer, thoroughly water the soil.

VARIETIES

• 'Camus de Bretagne': Large, well-flavoured heads; best in warm regions.
• 'Green Globe Improved': Widely grown, with large, globe-shaped, green heads.
• 'Purple Globe': Not with the best flavour, but ideal for planting in cold areas.
• 'Vert de Laon': One of the best and widely available.

Cardoons are grown for their fleshy, young stems which need to be blanched. Sow seeds in spring in groups of three, 45cm/18in apart. After germination, remove the weakest seedlings. Later, during late summer and early autumn, blanch stems by wrapping and tying black polythene around them. Stems are ready to lift after about five weeks.

1. GLOBE ARTICHOKES are best raised from suckers. In spring, cut suckers (about 20cm/8in long and with roots attached) from established plants. Plant them 60cm/2ft apart in rows 75cm/2½ft apart. Thoroughly water them.

2. DURING summer, regularly water plants and hoe between them to remove weeds. In late summer or early autumn, cut off the immature flower-heads, and in early winter cut all the stems down to ground level. Cover plants with straw.

3. IN THE following spring, remove the protective straw and dust a general fertilizer around the plants. From mid to late summer, cut off the fleshy flower-heads. In early winter, cut down stems and protect the plants with a layer of straw.

A R T I C H O K E S – J E R U S A L E M

❖

JERUSALEM Artichokes are completely different from Globe types: the Jerusalem ones are related to sunflowers and produce knobbly tubers which are harvested from late autumn to early spring.

Prepare the soil in autumn by digging in plenty of well-decomposed manure or garden compost. This ensures a supply of plant foods and retention of moisture.

Jerusalem Artichokes are easily grown, but do require support from stout stakes linked together with plastic-covered wires.

Plant tubers in late winter or early spring. Their main needs are watering throughout summer, especially during dry periods, and staking. Drawing up soil around their bases helps to prevent strong winds rocking plants and disturbing the roots. It also encourages the formation of young tubers near the surface. If the soil is light and impoverished, feed the plants with a liquid feed every three weeks during early and mid-summer.

Soil pests such as wireworms and slugs can be a problem; use slug baits and soil-pest chemicals.

When harvesting the tubers, retain a few for replanting during the following year. Ensure all tubers are dug up by spring; if left, they can be a nuisance when growing between other crops during the following summer.

The tubers are delicious made into soup, boiled, fried, baked, roasted or stewed.

VARIETIES

• 'Boston Red': Knobbly, with rosy-red skin.
• 'Fuseau': Perhaps the best variety, growing about 1.8/6ft high and with long, white tubers.
• 'Dwarf Sunray': Crisp and tender tubers, with plants 1.5m-2.4m/5-8ft high.
(Note: It is also possible to plant tubers bought from greengrocers and supermarkets.)

1. PLANT *tubers of Jerusalem Artichokes in early spring, 38cm/15in apart in drills 13–15cm/5–6in deep. When planting more than one row, space them 90cm/3ft apart. Water the soil thoroughly and keep it moist throughout summer.*

2. IN LATE SPRING, *after the tubers have sprouted and their positions can be seen, insert 2.4m/8ft-long canes along the row, with wire tied between them. Tie plants to these. When plants are 30cm/12in high, earth-up soil around their bases.*

3. AS SOON AS *the leaves turn brown in autumn, cut the stems about 20cm/8in above soil level. Leave the tubers in the ground, lifting them as needed between autumn and early spring. Keep back a few good tubers for replanting the next year.*

ASPARAGUS

❖

 ASPARAGUS is a long-term crop and often considered to be a luxury. But it is not difficult to grow and if there is space it is well worth establishing a bed of it. From planting one-year-old crowns in spring to being able to regularly cut asparagus spears takes two years. Once established, each plant can be expected to produce at least twenty spears each year. Asparagus beds have a life of between ten and twenty years, depending on how they are maintained: if the foliage is not cut down annually, the spears not cut and beds become blanketed in weeds, their life is very short. Additionally, asparagus beds have a longer life when in loamy to sandy soil than in clay, where the drainage is poor and plants may decay in winter. In these conditions, they are best grown in slightly raised beds.

Asparagus is an ideal crop to grow in coastal areas, in salty and light soil. However, it does need protection from cold winds.

RAISING PLANTS

Most gardeners buy one-year-old plants in spring, especially if only a few are needed. To raise your own, sow seeds outdoors in drills 12–18mm/½–¾in deep with the seeds 45cm/18in apart in early or mid-spring.

When the seedlings are established and growing strongly, thin them to 15cm/6in apart. During the following summer, pull up all weeds and ensure the soil does not become dry. In spring of the following year, plant the young crowns (see below). When planting, do not allow them to dry out: place them in a box lined with moist sacking or newspaper and keep covered.

If plants are left in a seed-bed for a further year, it is then possible to identify the female seed-bearing plants and to remove them (they are identified both by the seeds they bear and the seedlings which develop around them). The advantage in using only male plants is that, when planted in an asparagus bed,

1. IN SPRING, *dig a trench about 25cm/10in deep and 38cm/15in wide. Dust the base of the trench with a general fertilizer and lightly fork it in. At the same time, form and firm a mound along the base.*

2. BUY *one-year-old crowns and plant them 45cm/18in apart in the base of the trench. Spread out their roots and cover the crowns with 5cm/2in of friable soil. During summer, ensure that the soil is kept moist.*

3. IN LATE SUMMER *or early autumn, use sharp secateurs to cut down the stems to 7.5cm/3in above the soil's surface. Add a further layer of soil over the crowns to help protect them during winter.*

VARIETIES

• *'Connover's Colossal': Very popular and widely grown, developing early spears that are ideal for freezing.*
• *'Lorella': A good French variety with heavy crops of thick and succulent spears.*
• *'Martha Washington': An old and trusted variety, strong growing and producing heavy crops of long, thick spears. It is resistant to rust.*
• *'Minerve': Another French variety that shows great promise. The crops of spears are heavy and prolific.*
• *'Sutton's Perfection': A sturdy and resilient variety that is well established and reliable.*

LOOKING AFTER ASPARAGUS BEDS

During summer, keep the soil free from weeds and regularly water the beds. Each year, stems bearing fern-like leaves grow to about 1.2m/4ft high. In autumn, cut these down to 7.5cm/3in above the soil's surface.

In spring, dust the bed's surface with a general fertilizer and lightly fork it into the surface. Later, in the latter part of early summer and after the last spears have been cut, again dust the surface with a general fertilizer.

HARVESTING

Always use an asparagus knife to cut the spears. Wait until they are 13–15cm/5–6in above the soil and sever them about 5cm/2in below the surface. This job is best performed early in the morning when the spears are plump and full of moisture. When cutting mature spears, take care not to damage those that are small or have not yet broken through the soil's surface. After cutting the spears, water the bed to re-settle the soil.

removing unwanted seedlings is eliminated. However, one-year-old plants are much easier to establish than older ones and produce a more uniform crop than two-year-old plants which, by their nature, are variable in size. Always buy the best quality plants.

4. IN EARLY SPRING *of the following year, pull up all weeds and lightly fork between the rows. Dust with a general fertilizer and shallowly scratch it into the surface. Keep the bed moist and free from weeds.*

5. IN AUTUMN *of the second year, cut down the stems, remove all weeds and ridge up soil over the row. It is during the following year that the young spears can be harvested. Asparagus is a long-term crop.*

6. FROM LATE SPRING *to early or mid-summer of the following year, use an asparagus knife to cut the young spears when 13–15cm/5–6in high. Sever them about 5cm/2in below the soil's surface.*

BEANS – BROAD

❖

 THIS is a hardy vegetable that grows in most soils, especially those which are fertile and well drained but moisture-retentive. Dig the soil in early winter and add plenty of well-decomposed manure or compost. A sunny position is desirable, especially for early crops.

Sow seeds in double rows (see below) to produce the largest crops. Germination takes between one and two weeks and from a row 3m/10ft long about 9kg/20lbs of bean seeds can be expected.

HARVESTING

Early pods, when about 7.5cm/3in long, can be picked and cooked whole. But mainly the pods are harvested when the seeds inside them start to show through. The scar on each seed should be white or green, not discoloured. Pods are best picked with a twisting and downward pull.

After the complete crop has been picked, cut down the stems to ground level. Dig the roots into the soil well.

VARIETIES

Long-pod broad beans
Narrow pods about 38cm/15in long. Hardy, with high yields.
• *'Aquadulce Claudia': White seeded and early cropping.*
• *'Hylon': New variety with long pods and white seeds.*
• *'Imperial Green Longpod': High yields and green seeds.*
• *'Imperial White Longpod': An old variety with white seeds.*
• *'Relon': Pods more than 50cm/20in long and packed with green seeds.*

Windsor broad beans
Shorter pods, each with up to seven beans. They are known for their superb flavour.
• *'Green Windsor': Heavy cropping with green seeds.*
• *'White Windsor': White seeds.*

Dwarf broad beans
Plants grow 30–45cm/12–15in high and are ideal for windy sites, small gardens and under cloches.
• *'The Sutton': White, superbly flavoured seeds.*

1. IN EARLY SPRING, *form drills 7.5cm/3in deep and in pairs 30cm/12in apart. Space these pairs 60cm/2ft apart. Sow bean seeds 23cm/9in apart in each drill, cover and firm soil over them.*

2. SUPPORT *plants by inserting strong posts at each corner of the double row and tying strong string around them, 38–45cm/15–18in above the ground. For long rows, supporting sticks half-way along are needed.*

3. WHEN *plants are in full flower, pinch out the top of each shoot. This encourages the uniform development of pods on plants, as well as reducing the risk of an infestation of the black bean aphid.*

BEANS – FRENCH

❖

THESE have always been popular, although not to the same extent as Runner Beans. However, they have many advantages in small or exposed gardens. There are climbing forms and varieties include 'Blue Lake' (pencil-shaped pods on plants that grow up to 1.5m/5ft high).

The seeds germinate within one to two weeks of being sown, and the normal yield for dwarf types is 3.5kg/8lb for every 3m/10ft of row. Climbing forms yield more, about 5.5kg/12lb for every 3m/10ft of the row.

LOOKING AFTER THE PLANTS

Slugs attack bean seedlings, so use baits around them. Plants are nearly self-supporting, but benefit from twiggy sticks pushed among them; this is necessary when plants are cropping heavily, and also during wet weather.

Support climbing types with string or form a wigwam of bamboo canes. Netting can also be used to support the plants.

VARIETIES

The range of dwarf French Beans is wide and includes:
- *'Masterpiece': Flat pods.*
- *'Tendergreen': Pencil podded.*
- *'The Prince': Popular and with flat pods.*
- *'Royal Burgundy': Purple, pencil-shaped pods.*

GROW EARLY *crops of dwarf French Beans by lightly forking soil in late winter and placing barn cloches over the row. In mid-spring, when the soil has warmed up, sow seeds (described below). Keep the soil moist and pick pods in early summer.*

1. IN LATE SPRING *or early summer, form drills 5cm/2in deep and 45cm/18in apart. Sow the individual seeds 7.5–10cm/ 3–4in apart. A sunny position and fertile, moisture-retentive soil assures success.*

2. IN EARLY SUMMER, *hoe between rows to remove weeds and to break up crusty surfaces. Thoroughly water the soil and form a mulch around the plants to conserve moisture and to keep the roots cool.*

3. FROM MID-SUMMER *onwards, pick the pods when young, usually initially about 13cm/5in long. To show their freshness they should snap in half when bent. Regularly picking them encourages further beans.*

BEANS – RUNNER

❖

RUNNER beans are one of the best known vegetables. They are easily grown and seeds can be sown in the positions where they are to grow. The essential elements for growing them are sunshine and soil that does not dry out. It is not possible to guarantee sunshine, other than positioning plants in a sunny, wind-sheltered position, but moisture in the soil can be encouraged by digging in plenty of well-decomposed garden compost or manure in late winter. Also, regularly watering the soil and forming a 7.5cm/3in mulch around plants helps in the retention of moisture. Apart from their food value, a row of beans can be used to form a peep-proof screen; it is especially attractive when in flower.

SOWING OR PLANTING

The majority of runner beans are raised by sowing their seeds in the positions in which they will grow. The precise time to sow them depends on the risk of frost, as young bean plants are soon killed by low temperatures.

An alternative way – and to produce a slightly earlier crop – is to buy established plants and to plant them as soon as all risk of frost has passed. Indeed, in cold areas, this method is especially advised. When growing beans in this way, erect the supports before setting the young plants in position. It is then easier to estimate the exact number of plants needed. It also prevents the roots of plants being disturbed by the poles.

1. IN EARLY SPRING, *dig a trench about 25cm/10in deep and 75cm/2½ft wide. Fork the bottom and mix in well-decayed manure or garden compost to both feed plants and assist in the retention of moisture around their roots. Refill the trench with soil. At this stage the surface will be slightly mounded, but will settle.*

2. IN LATE SPRING *(in mild areas) or early summer (for cold regions) sow seeds. It is essential that seedlings should not be exposed to frost. Use a draw hoe to form two 5cm/2in-deep drills, 60cm/2ft apart. Sow seeds in them, 15cm/6in apart. Cover them with soil and firm it. Keep the soil moist but not waterlogged.*

3. DURING *germination, which takes up to two weeks, it is essential to keep the soil moist and free from weeds. After germination and until the plants are about 10cm/4in high the additional problem is slugs. Unless deterred by baits they can devastate a row of young bean plants overnight in warm, wet weather.*

VARIETIES

- *'Desiree'*: A stringless variety producing about forty pods on each plant. Unlike most varieties, it is excellent, even in dry summers.
- *'Erecta'*: Widely grown commercially, it is very tolerant of growing conditions and produces pods up to 38cm/15in long.
- *'Kelvedon Marvel'*: Long, straight pods, up to 30cm/12in long. Ideal for freezing.
- *'Mergoles'*: A stringless variety with slightly curved pods borne in large clusters.
- *'Scarlet Emperor'*: Heavy cropping, with smooth-textured pods. Ideal for eating and exhibiting.
- *'Streamline'*: Deliciously flavoured pods up to 40cm/16in.
- *'Sunset'*: Perhaps the earliest variety, with good-flavoured pods.

SURVIVING GLUTS OF BEANS

Unless you have a large family with an insatiable appetite for runner beans it is almost impossible to avoid times when there are too many beans. Even in times of glut it is not wise to abandon picking for several days, as beans will become tough and old. Also, it will prevent the development of other beans. Therefore, the solution is to store or freeze them.

Storing them loose is only possible for up to about a week: pack the pods in polythene bags and place in a refrigerator. Freezing is a better solution, when they last for up to a year. Pick young, healthy beans early in the morning, when they are fresh, and wash, trim and slice them into chunks. Dip them in boiling water for two minutes and cool rapidly. Allow water to drain, then dry them and place in labelled freezer bags.

 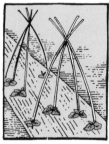 

4. WHEN *bean plants are about 10cm/4in high, erect supports 1.8–2.4m/6–8ft high. Bean poles inserted along the outer sides of the double row, and 15–30cm/6–12in apart, is the traditional method of supporting plants. Angle the poles inwards, cross their tops and tie a horizontal pole to them securely.*

5. ALTERNATIVE *ways to support runner beans include tripods of poles (sometimes four poles are used). These are ideal where space prevents the erection of long rows of bean poles. Another way is to use strings secured by wire hooks in the ground and tied to a cross-bar at the top. It is essential that these supports are strong.*

6. HARVEST *beans as soon as they are large enough to be eaten – do not wait until they are tough. Regular picking is essential to encourage the formation of further beans. A 3m/10ft-long row will yield about 27kg/60lb of beans. They can be eaten fresh, or blanched, cooled and placed in a freezer.*

BEETROOT

❖

BEETROOTS are sown in spring and harvested throughout summer for immediate use, or stored in boxes of dry sand or peat for eating during winter and up to early spring. Stagger sowings between spring and early summer to provide young roots throughout summer.

VARIETIES

Globe beetroot
Round and quick maturing.
• *'Boltardy': Resistant to developing seed-heads when sown early. Sweet, deep red flesh with a fresh flavour.*
• *'Burpee's Golden': Superb flavour, with yellow flesh that does not bleed.*
• *'Detroit': Ideal as a main crop variety, with red flesh. Can be stored throughout winter.*
• *'Monopoly': Each seed cluster produces only one seedling, thereby eliminating thinning. Resistant to bolting. Red flesh.*
Cylindrical beetroot
Ideal for storing.
• *'Cylindra': Deep red flesh. Keeps well*
Long beetroot
Deep soil is essential.
• *'Cheltenham Green Top': Popular with exhibitors.*

STORING BEETROOT

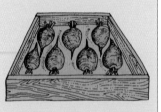

Ensure the leaves have been twisted off 5cm/2in above the crown. Also, pull off dead or decaying leaves. Then, pack dry sand or peat around them and place in a cool, vermin-proof shed or cellar.

1. DIG THE SOIL *in late winter but do not add manure or lime. In spring shallowly fork the soil, rake to a fine tilth and form drills 2.5cm/1in deep and 30cm/12in apart. Sow seeds in clusters of three, 10–15cm/4–6in apart.*

2. WHEN *the seedlings have formed their first leaves, other than their original seed-leaves, thin them to one seedling at each position. Re-firm soil around the remaining seedlings, then water them gently but thoroughly.*

3. IN LATE SUMMER, *use a garden fork to break the soil under each beetroot. Gently ease them from the soil without bruising the skin. Either use them immediately or carefully twist off the leaves (5cm/ 2in above the crown).*

BROCCOLI
AND CALABRESE
❖

THESE two vegetables are increasing in popularity. They are quite similar: purple and white broccoli varieties have small, leafy flowers on short stalks, while calabrese is often known as green sprouting broccoli. Broccoli mainly matures from mid-winter to late spring, whereas calabrese is ready for cutting in autumn.

RAISING AND LOOKING AFTER PLANTS

Both broccoli and calabrese are raised in the same way, initially in seed-beds and then transplanted when 7.5cm/3in high to their growing positions. Treat the plants against club-root when setting them in the soil.

Protect young plants from birds and keep the soil moist. For broccoli, draw up soil around their stems in late summer to support them in exposed sites.

VARIETIES

Broccoli
• *'Christmas Purple Sprouting'*: An ideal variety for harvesting in mid-winter.
• *'Early Purple Sprouting'*: Sow in late spring for harvesting in early spring of the following year.
• *'White Sprouting'*: Sow in late spring for harvesting in late spring of the following year.

Calabrese varieties
• *'Calabrese Green Sprouting'*: Sow in early to late spring for harvesting the crop in late summer or autumn.
• *'Green Comet'*: Sow in early spring for harvesting them from summer to autumn.
• *'Romanesco'*: Sow in early to late spring for harvesting in late summer or autumn.

1. PREPARE *a seed-bed (see pages 14 and 15) in spring and sow seeds evenly and thinly in drills 12mm/ ½in deep and 20cm/8in apart. Keep the seed-bed well watered and free from weeds. Also, sow seeds in early summer.*

2. IN EARLY SUMMER, *transplant early sown seedlings. For later sowings, this will be about mid-summer. Water seed-beds and planting positions the day before and space plants 45cm/1½ft apart in rows a similar distance apart.*

3. HARVEST *the central heads when mature, cutting them with a sharp knife. To assist in the development of sideshoots, water the plants with a general fertilizer. Later, the sideshoots can be harvested. when they form good-sized heads.*

BRUSSELS SPROUTS

❖

 BRUSSELS sprouts are an important and popular crop. By selecting the right varieties, sprouts can be ready for harvesting from late summer to early spring (see the opposite page for suitable varieties). The main disappointment with them is 'blown' sprouts, but this can be overcome by careful soil preparation and planting (see right for the cause).

The other hazard with Brussels sprouts is cooking them for too long. Everyone has their own idea of when food has been cooked sufficiently, but sprouts are soon made soggy and unappealing by excess cooking.

BLOWN SPROUTS

Occasionally, sprouts open prematurely and become leafy instead of remaining as tight buttons. This is caused by insufficient organic material such as garden compost and manure being added to the soil. If the soil is loose and has not been firmed (see below) this, too, contributes to the problem. Loose planting is another cause of this problem; to test if plants are firmly in the soil, part of a leaf when pulled should come away and not disturb the roots.

RAISING PLANTS

Prepare a seed-bed in late winter. In early to mid-spring, sow seeds thinly and evenly, 12–18mm/ ¹/₂–³/₄in deep in drills about 15–20cm/6–8in apart. Germination takes up to twelve days. Keep the seed-bed moist and when the seedlings are large enough to handle, thin them to about 7.5cm/3in apart. When the young plants are 10–13cm/4–5in high, transplant them to their growing positions (see below). Set the plants with their lowest leaves fractionally above the surface.

 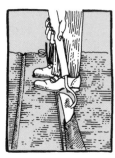 

1. DIG THE SOIL *in early winter, adding manure or compost, especially if it is light and sandy. In late winter, apply lime so that the soil is slightly alkaline (see pages 12 and 13). In early spring, rake and firm the soil ready for sowing seeds.*

2. AFTER *raking and treading the soil, again rake it to remove foot prints that might trap rain and cause puddles. Use a garden line and draw hoe to form drills 5cm/2in deep and 60–75cm/2–2¹/₂ft apart. Plants are planted in them.*

3. DURING *late spring and early summer, transplant plants earlier raised in a seed-bed. Planting in drills conserves moisture around their roots; if the soil is moisture retentive, the V-drills are not necessary. Water each plant.*

HARVESTING AND 'GLUTS'

Always start picking the buttons from the base of the stem upwards. At this stage, the sprouts should be tight and about the size of a walnut. Do not wait until the leaves surrounding them become loose. Remove sprouts from the stem by forcing them downwards with a sudden push. Alternatively, use a sharp knife. It may take several weeks before each plant has been totally cleared of sprouts.

Fresh sprouts are a culinary delight, but often – and especially when F1 hybrids are grown – too many of them are ready for harvesting at one time. Do not leave them on the plants, as they will spoil. Wash, dry and pack them in polythene bags and place in a refrigerator for up to five days.

For longer periods freezing is necessary. Wash, strip off loose outer leaves and soak them in water for about twenty minutes. Then, blanch for three minutes, cool rapidly, dry and place in freezer bags. Seal the bags, label and place in a freezer.

VARIETIES

The two main types of varieties are the standard (traditional ones) and newer F1 types.

Standard Brussels Sprouts

• *'Bedford Fillbasket': Heavy crops of large, solid sprouts from early autumn to Christmas.*
• *'Cambridge No. 5': High quality, walnut-sized sprouts from Christmas to early spring.*

F1 Brussels Sprouts

These varieties produce uniform buttons, ready for harvesting all at the same time.
• *'Citadel': Tight, firm sprouts from mid-winter to mid-spring.*
• *'Icarus F1': Large crops of solid, sweet buttons. It is resistant to cold and ready for harvesting from mid-autumn to late winter.*
• *'Peer Gynt': Prolific cropping from mid-autumn to early winter.*
• *'Stabolite': Ideal in cold climates. Picking from mid-winter to early spring.*

4. DURING *mid-summer, use a draw hoe to pull up a little soil around the base of each stem. Also, remove weeds and keep the soil moist but not waterlogged, especially when the plants are young. Ensure birds do not pull off leaves.*

5. PLANTS *benefit from a foliar feed (high in potash) in the latter part of mid-summer. This rapidly stimulates growth during the late summer and into early autumn without making plants soft and susceptible to low termperatures.*

6. THE BUTTONS *can be harvested as soon as they are firm, which is usually from autumn to late winter, depending on the variety (see above). To prevent tall varieties being blown over, draw further soil up around the base of each stem.*

CABBAGES

❖

THERE is a wide range of cabbages and they are ready for eating throughout the year. The main types are discussed here, together with their sowing, planting and harvesting times. It is essential to select the right type, especially for those grown during winter, when hardy varieties are particularly essential.

Cabbages are easily raised from seeds, but if only a few plants are needed, it is easier to buy them from a local nursery.

SPRING CABBAGES
Conical and initially provide 'spring greens', later heads.
- *Sow seeds: Mid to late summer. Sow thinly and pull early plants for spring greens. Leave others to mature.*
- *Planting: Autumn.*
- *Harvesting: Mid and late spring, sometimes slightly earlier.*
- *Varieties: 'April', 'Durham Early' and 'Offenham – Flower of Spring'.*

SUMMER CABBAGES
These are generally ball shaped.
- *Sow seeds: Mid-spring (or slightly earlier when sown under cloches).*
- *Planting: Late spring and early summer. Space plants 45–60cm/ 1½–2ft apart each way.*
- *Harvesting: Late summer and early autumn.*
- *Varieties: 'Greyhound', 'Hispi', 'Minicole', 'Primo' and 'Winnigstadt'.*

WINTER CABBAGES
These are usually drum or ball headed and either green or white.
- *Sow seeds: Mid and late spring.*
- *Planting: Latter part of early summer and through mid-summer. Space plants 60cm/2ft apart each way.*
- *Harvesting: Early to late winter.*
- *Varieties: 'Celtic', 'Christmas Drumhead', 'January King' and 'Jupiter'.*

SAVOY CABBAGES
These have distinctively puckered and crisp, dark green leaves.
- *Sow: Mid and late spring.*
- *Planting: Mid-summer. Space plants 60m/2ft apart each way.*
- *Harvesting: Late autumn to late winter.*
- *Varieties: 'Best of All', 'Ormskirk Late', 'Savoy King' and 'Ormskirk Rearguard'. This last variety is especially recommended when seeking a cabbage to cut at Christmas.*

Through the centuries, cabbages have been unjustifiably maligned and the butt of schoolboy jokes. But for many years they were a staple food of country folk, and if properly cooked have a superb flavour and crispness. It is when they are boiled 'all morning' that cabbages lose their appeal and become tasteless.

As a change, both red and white cabbages can be chopped and eaten raw in salads. Stir-fried Chinese cabbage, or leaves stuffed with minced meat, are other ways to use them. Cabbages can be frozen, but as they are available throughout the year it is best to use freezer space for vegetables with a shorter harvesting season.

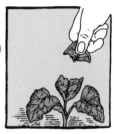

1. YOUNG *cabbage plants are raised in seed-beds (see pages 14 and 15). The time of sowing depends on the cabbage (see below and on the opposite page). Sow seeds 12mm/½in deep, later thinning the plants to 7.5cm/3in apart.*

2. WHEN *the plants have four or five leaves, transplant them to the vegetable plot. Water the seed-bed and the garden the day before to ensure the young plants become established quickly. Use a dibber to plant them firmly in the soil.*

3. IF CLUB-ROOT *is prevalent, dip the roots in thiophanate-methyl. To check if the plants are firmly planted, pull part of a leaf. It should tear away and leave the plant's roots undisturbed. Water the plants thoroughly.*

CHINESE CABBAGES
Tall and cylindrical and more like a cos lettuce than a cabbage.
- *Sow: Mid-summer (sometimes slightly earlier for some varieties), in drills 30cm/12in apart. Space the seeds 10cm/4in apart and later thin to 30cm/12in between plants. Do not transplant Chinese cabbages. Water well during dry periods.*
- *Harvest: Early and mid-autumn.*
- *Varieties: 'Tip-top', 'Kasumi', 'Sampan' and 'Two Seasons'.*

RED CABBAGES
Distinctive, with rich, red leaves. It is widely grown for pickling, but can also be boiled and eaten in the same way as other, more ordinary cabbages.
- *Sow: Mid-spring.*
- *Planting: Later spring and early summer. Space plants 60cm/2ft each way.*
- *Harvesting: Early and mid-autumn.*
- *Varieties: 'Red Drumhead' and 'Stockley's Giant Red'.*

CAULIFLOWERS

❖

CAULIFLOWERS are popular and widely grown. There are three types – winter, summer and autumn – and between them they provide edible heads, called curds, throughout much of the year.

RAISING YOUNG PLANTS

All three types of cauliflower can be raised by sowing seeds in a seed-bed in spring, but to produce early 'summer' types it is necessary to raise plants in gentle warmth (13°C/55°F) in a greenhouse in mid-winter. Reduce the temperature after germination and prick out the seedlings into cold frames, setting them about 7.5cm/3in square. Plant them into gardens in early spring. Raising plants in seed-beds outdoors is detailed below.

Whether in the greenhouse or outdoors, sow seeds thinly.

LOOKING AFTER PLANTS

Dig the soil thoroughly during early winter and mix in garden compost or manure that is well decayed. In late winter check that the soil is slightly alkaline and, later, a couple of weeks before planting, dust and thoroughly rake in a good general-purpose fertilizer.

Regularly watering plants is essential, as growth is dramatically reduced during droughts and the curds do not subsequently develop to their full size. Always thoroughly water the soil; just dampening the surface does more harm than good.

Birds are frequently a nuisance to young plants and if they are persistent, wire-netting hoops may be needed to protect them.

On light soils, where nutrients are soon leached away, feed summer types in mid-summer. Do not feed the others, as it will make growth too soft for winter survival.

1. SOW SEEDS *in a seed-bed during mid and late spring, in drills 12mm/½in deep and 15–20cm/6–8in apart. Germination takes up to twelve days. Thin the seedlings 7.5cm/3in apart.*

2. WHEN *young cauliflower plants have about five leaves they can be moved to their growing positions. Water the seed-bed and planting positions the day before moving them and lift the young plants with care.*

3. BEFORE *planting, dip their roots in a fungicide that will prevent an incidence of club-root. Plant them firmly, setting summer and autumn varieties approximately 60cm/2ft apart, and winter varieties 75cm/2½ft.*

VARIETIES

Summer cauliflowers
These are ready for cutting from mid-summer to early autumn.
- *'All The Year Round': Can be sown in gentle warmth in mid-winter, or outdoors during spring.*
- *'Dok-Elgon': Late-summer variety.*
- *'Snowball': An ideal early variety.*

Autumn cauliflowers
Ready for harvesting in autumn and early winter.
- *'Autumn Giant': Large heads in early winter.*
- *'Canberra': Matures in early winter.*
- *'Barrier Reef': Ideal in late autumn and early winter.*

Winter cauliflowers
These are ready for cutting from early winter to late spring.
- *'Late Queen': Ideal for cutting in late spring.*
- *'Snow's Winter White': Tolerant of cold weather and easily grown.*

MINI-CAULIFLOWERS

These are easily grown and are increasing in popularity. They are grown by sowing seeds where the small cauliflowers are to grow. And as they are grown close together, in a space about 15cm/6in square, it means they are ideal for small gardens. Additionally, because of their size – about 7.5cm/3in across – they are easily frozen for use later.

Sow seeds thinly and evenly in mid-spring, about 12mm/½in deep and in drills 15cm/6in apart. When the seedlings are large enough to handle, thin them first to 7.5cm/3in apart, later to 15cm/6in. By making two further sowings at three-week intervals, mini-cauliflowers can be cut from mid-summer to late autumn.

Suitable varieties include:
- 'Cargill Early Maturing Variety': For early sowing.
- 'Garant' (early-maturing variety): For early sowings, where the heads do not mature all at the same time.
- 'Predominant' (late-maturing variety): Ideal for later sowings and for freezing.

4. WHEN *planting, firm the soil around and over the roots and leave a small depression on the surface around each plant. This then can be filled with water to ensure soil settles around the roots. Water them several times.*

5. BEND *a few leaves over summer-maturing varieties to prevent sun bleaching and drying the curds. Also, by folding leaves over winter types they can be protected from snow and frost. Wait until frost is imminent.*

6. USE *a sharp knife to harvest cauliflowers. The curds should be firm and well developed but not open. Cut summer-maturing types usually in the late morning, and winter ones as soon as frost has left them.*

CARROTS

❖

 CARROTS are a very versatile vegetable and deserve to be more widely grown. They are equally superb when grated in salads, cooked in stews or served as a hot vegetable. Long-rooted exhibition varieties need very deep, well-prepared soil. But generally, it is the shorter-rooted types that are grown for home use.

SOWING AND LOOKING AFTER PLANTS

Sowing carrots is detailed below, while the main task when growing them is removing weeds, hoeing between the rows and ensuring the soil does not become dry.

The most devastating pest is carrot root-fly (pages 58 and 59). Risk of attack can be reduced by sowing seeds thinly. To mask the smell (which carrot flies are said to be able to detect from more than a mile away) place paraffin-soaked rags between the rows, or plant onions or garlic alongside them to disguise the smell.

VARIETIES

<u>Short-rooted carrots</u>
Finger-like, or resembling small golf balls; sow this variety every two weeks from spring to mid-summer.
• *'Amsterdam Forcing': Early variety, with stump-end roots.*
• *'Kundulus': Short and cylindrical, almost like a ball.*
<u>Intermediate-rooted carrots</u>
Medium-sized roots, usually sown slightly later than the short-rooted types for harvesting when young or left to mature.
• *'Autumn King Improved': Long, but still stump-rooted.*
• *'Mokum': Matures quickly; sow from spring to mid-summer.*
<u>Long-rooted carrots</u>
Long, tapering roots requiring deep, well-cultivated soil.
• *'New Red Intermediate': Long roots that store well.*
• *'St. Valery': Long roots, often used by exhibitors.*

1. FROM MID-SPRING *to the latter part of early summer, sow seeds outdoors in drills 12–18mm/ ½–¾in deep and 15cm/6in apart. Cover and firm the drills, then water thoroughly but gently. If carrots are deprived of moisture they become woody.*

2. THIN THE SEEDLINGS *when they are large enough to handle, spacing them about 6cm/ 2½in apart. Pick up and burn all thinnings, as they attract carrot flies. Re-firm soil around the carrot seedlings that remain and thoroughly water the soil.*

3. AS SOON AS *young carrots are large enough to be eaten, pull them up. At this stage they will be succulent and tender. Later, when lifting roots for storage, it is necessary to use a garden fork. Twist off the foliage, just above the roots. Take care not to bruise them.*

CUCUMBERS – OUTDOOR

❖

OUTDOOR cucumbers, also known as ridge types, are easy to grow but do need a warm, sunny, position that is wind sheltered, and plenty of water during summer.

PREPARING THE SOIL

In mid-spring, dig holes about 30cm/12in deep and 38cm/15in wide and fill them with a mixture of friable soil and decomposed garden compost or manure. Replace the rest of the soil to form a mound. Sow seeds as soon as all risk of frost has passed (detailed below). If more than one mound is formed, space them 90cm/3ft apart.

GROWING, TRAINING AND HARVESTING

Once the seeds have germinated, remove the growing tips from the shoots, spreading them out so that sideshoots can grow. If these do not develop flowers, carefully nip off the tips beyond the sixth leaf.

VARIETIES

- *'Burpless Tasty Green'*: Tasty and with no bitterness.
- *'Chinese Long Green'*: Japanese variety with long fruits and smooth skin.
- *'Kyoto'*: Japanese variety with long, straight, smooth-skinned fruits.
- *'Sweet Success'*: An 'all-female' type and therefore not producing vast amounts of seed.
- *'Zeppelin'*: Large fruits.

From the latter part of mid-summer, use a sharp knife to cut the cucumbers when 15–20cm/6–8in long. Do not leave them to grow further as this discourages the development of further fruits.

Harvesting stops instantaneously with the first frosts of autumn. However, if the fruits are picked while young and plants watered and fed regularly it is possible to produce a large crop.

1. PREPARE *the planting mound in mid-spring, as detailed above. In late spring in warm areas, and early summer where late frosts are likely, sow three seeds 18mm/⅜in deep and 5cm/2in apart, in a triangle. Water and cover with a large jam jar.*

2. KEEP *the soil moist, and after germination, when the seedlings have several leaves, remove the weakest seedlings to leave one strong plant on each mound. Firm soil around the remaining plant and gently water it. After about a week, carefully remove the jam jar.*

3. DURING *early and mid-summer the plant will develop sideshoots. When these have five or six leaves, pinch out their tips just beyond a leaf. Water plants regularly and feed them with a weak liquid fertilizer as soon as the first fruits start to swell.*

CELERY

❖

CELERY is grown for its blanched leaf stalks and can be used in several ways, including fresh in salads or braised as a vegetable. Fertile, moisture-retentive soil with plenty of garden compost or manure is essential to encourage strong and rapid growth. Additionally, the total exclusion of light by either earthing-up trench celery or growing self-blanching types close together is vital for producing a good crop.

EARTHING-UP

Before earthing-up trench celery, tie the tops of their stems together to prevent soil falling between them. Wrapping newspaper or corrugated cardboard around the stems keeps them clean, but may encourage pests to linger. Never completely cover the leaves at each earthing-up, and afterwards water the plants so that soil settles around the stem but never into the heart. It is better to earth-up the plants several times than to do it just once, and to damage them.

RAISING YOUNG PLANTS

Raise new plants by sowing seeds in gentle warmth (13–15°C/ 55–59°F) in early or mid-spring. After germination, reduce the temperature slightly and when the seedlings are large enough to handle, prick them out into seed-trays, setting them about 5cm/2in apart. Slowly acclimatise the plants to outdoor conditions, taking care that the compost does not become dry. In late spring or early summer plant them out.

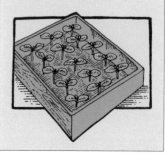

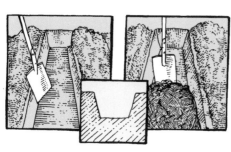

1. IN EARLY SPRING, *select a well-drained piece of soil and dig a trench 38cm/15in wide and 25–30cm/10–12in deep. Place excavated soil along the sides. If there is more than one trench, space them about 1.2m/4ft apart.*

2. USE A GARDEN *fork or spade to mix plenty of well-decayed garden compost or manure into the base of the trench. Add more garden compost and mix it with further soil until within 7.5cm/3in of the surface. Then, leave the area open.*

3. A WEEK *before setting the plants in position in late spring or early summer, dust the trench's surface with a general fertilizer. Set the plants in two staggered rows 23cm/9in apart with the same distance between the individual plants.*

SELF-BLANCHING CELERY

This type is easier to grow than the 'trench' form, as it is not necessary to dig a trench. It is best grown in a cold frame – no glass covering is needed – so that light is excluded from the edges of the block of plants. Self-blanching celery is not so hardy as trench type, which can be left in the soil and harvested over a long period. Some varieties of trench celery can be harvested in late winter. The self-blanching type, however, is best eaten soon after it is harvested, from late summer and late autumn. Both types need copious amounts of water during summer.

DURING late winter or early spring, fork over soil in a cold frame and add garden compost or well-decomposed manure. In late spring or early summer, rake and level the surface. Mark the surface into 23cm/9in squares and put in the young plants. Thoroughly water the plants.

FROM late summer to late autumn, use a trowel or garden fork to lift the plants. Wash them and, preferably, eat immediately. After digging up a few plants, pack straw around those that remain to prevent the stems becoming tough and green.

VARIETIES

Trench celery
• 'Giant Pink': Crisp, pink sticks, ideal for use during mid and late winter.
• 'Giant Red': Purplish green sticks, turning shell pink when blanched.
• 'Giant White': Well-known and widely grown white variety.

Self-blanching celery
• 'American Queen': Widely grown, green and stringless.
• 'Celebrity': Long sticks.
• 'Golden Self-blanching': Early maturing, with yellow sticks.
• 'Lathom Self-blanching': Good flavoured, yellow variety.

4. WATER the young plants and during mid-summer, when they are 25–30cm/10–12in high, tie the stems together just below the leaves. Every three weeks, trickle some soil around the plants (earthing-up), to blanch the stems.

5. AS PLANTS grow and their stems lengthen, continue to mound up soil. This is best done after a shower of rain. If plants are earthed-up when the soil is dry the leaves of plants form an umbrella and never allow it to become moist.

6. FROM late autumn to late winter dig up trench celery, wash and eat it. Use a trowel, although if plants are deeply rooted a garden fork is needed. Cover plants with straw in winter to prevent the soil being frozen and to keep them balanced.

LETTUCE

❖

 LETTUCE is by far the most popular salad crop, with a wide range of types, sowing and harvesting times. Most are raised without the need for cloches or frames, but those that grow through winter need protection (see opposite page).

Growing lettuces requires three basic factors: the soil must be fertile and contain well-decomposed garden compost, both to feed the plants and assist in the retention of moisture; plants must be regularly watered; and the soil must not be acid, a pH of 6.5–7.5 being desirable (see pages 12 and 13 for correcting acidity). A sunny or lightly shaded site is an advantage.

Slugs, snails and greenfly are the main pests likely to infest lettuces and unless they are controlled, crops are soon decimated (see pages 58 and 59).

BUTTERHEAD LETTUCE *is a cabbage type, with large, soft and smooth-edged leaves. Varieties include:*
- *'All the Year Round'*
- *'Arctic King'*
- *'Buttercrunch'*
- *'Dolly'* • *'Tom Thumb'*

CRISPHEAD LETTUCE *is another cabbage type, with rounded heads with curled and crisp leaves. Varieties include:*
- *'Avoncrisp'*
- *'Great Lakes'* • *'Iceberg'*
- *'Webb's Wonderful'*

COS LETTUCES *differ dramatically from cabbage types and have upright growth and oblong heads. Varieties include:*
- *'Barcarolle'* • *'Little Gem'*
- *'Lobjoit's Green'*
- *'Winter Density'*

SPRING LETTUCE

1. SOW SPRING *lettuce in mild areas in the latter part of late summer or early autumn to produce lettuces for cutting in late spring. Sow seeds 12mm/½in deep in drills 25cm/10in apart. Use c variety that is winter-hardy.*

2. 'ARCTIC KING', *'Valdor' or 'All The Year Round' are suitable varieties. When the seedlings are 18mm/¾in high (during early to mid-autumn) thin them to 5–7.5cm/2–3in apart. Then, carefully hoe between the rows.*

3. IN LATE WINTER *or early spring, again thin the seedlings, this time to 23–30cm/9–12in apart, depending on the variety but usually 30cm/12in. At the same time, dust and hoe a general fertilizer into the surface soil.*

SUMMER LETTUCE

1. SOW SUMMER *lettuce from mid-spring to the early part of late summer in drills 12mm/½in deep and 25cm/10in apart. Sow the seeds evenly and thinly, then cover with friable soil. Keep the seed-bed moist but not excessively wet.*

2. WHEN THE *seedlings are about 2.5cm/1in high, thin them first to 10cm/4in apart, later to 30cm/12in. Small varieties, however, need only be thinned to 20cm/8in apart. Regularly water the seedlings to ensure they grow steadily and rapidly.*

3. FROM THE *latter part of early summer to autumn, harvest the lettuces. Test the hearts for firmness by pressing with the back of a hand, not with fingers which may cause bruising. Use a knife to cut the stem below the lowest leaf.*

UNDER CLOCHES

By sowing seeds in mid-autumn and covering the seedlings with cloches, lettuces can be harvested in early and mid-spring.

Sow three seeds 12mm/½in deep and 7.5cm/3in apart in rows 20cm/8in apart, then place cloches over them. Ensure the cloches and their ends are very well secured.

In mid-autumn, when the seedlings are about 18mm/¾in high, thin them so that you leave just the strongest seedling in each group. Ventilate the cloches in winter, but avoid draughts. During late winter, thin the seedlings to 23cm/9in apart and keep the soil evenly moist. Dwarf varieties are thinned to 15cm/6in apart.

LOOSE-LEAF LETTUCES

These are sometimes known as loose-head types and they differ from normal lettuces in having masses of loose, wavy leaves which can be picked over several weeks. Varieties include 'Salad Bowl' and 'Red Salad Bowl'.

Sow seeds thinly and evenly 12mm/½in deep and in drills 13cm/5in apart during late spring and early summer. Do not thin the seedlings, and harvest the leaves about six weeks after sowing them. Use a sharp knife to cut off the leaves slightly above soil level. Leave the stumps to produce a further crop. Ensure that the soil is kept moist, but not waterlogged.

LEEKS

Leeks can be harvested in early autumn, but mostly they are a winter crop. The choice of varieties is important and a range of suitable varieties for early, mid-season and late crops is shown here. Although large, fat leeks are usually grown for exhibition purposes, small ones are better suited for home use. Indeed, the flavour and tenderness usually decreases as size increases.

CULTIVATION AND HARVESTING

When planting, never fill the hole with soil; just pop in the young plant and water it thoroughly. Leeks are gross feeders, but do not feed them after late summer as it diminishes the ability of mid and late-season varieties to survive low temperatures in winter. Use a draw hoe to pull up soil around the plants several times during a season, but take care not to allow it to fall between the leaves.

Use a garden fork to dig under and to harvest the plants.

VARIETIES

Leek varieties can be arranged into three groups, according to the times they are harvested.

Early leeks
Ready for harvesting from early autumn to early winter.
• 'Early Market'
• 'The Lyon - Prizetaker'
• 'Walton Mammoth'

Mid-season leeks
For harvesting early to late winter.
• 'King Richard'
• 'Molos': For harvesting late autumn to mid-winter.
• 'Musselburgh Improved'

Late season leeks
Ready for harvesting from late winter to mid-spring.
• 'Giant Winter-Royal Favourite'.
• 'Winter Crop': Ideal in very cold and exposed areas.
• 'Yates Empire': Does not suffer by being left in the ground.

1. DURING EARLY *to mid-spring, sow seeds thinely and evenly, 12mm/½in deep and in rows 15cm/6in apart in a seed-bed. Keep the soil moist and free from weeds. Thin the seedlings to 3.6–5cm/1½–2in apart and re-firm loosened soil.*

2. WHEN PLANTS *are about 20cm/8in high, use a dibber to form holes 15cm/6in deep and 15cm/6in apart in rows 30cm/12in apart. Trim off one-third of the roots and leaves and drop a plant into each hole. Just fill the hole with water.*

3. DURING *summer, keep the soil moist and mulch the plants. Once plants are well developed, draw soil around them to create a larger blanched area. Feed leeks until late summer, and harvest them from early autumn to spring.*

MARROWS
❖

THESE fleshy-fruited vegetables are increasingly popular, together with courgettes, which are really small marrows. Indeed, some varieties, such as the popular 'Green Bush' can be grown as both.

RAISING YOUNG PLANTS
Young plants can be raised by sowing seeds where they are to grow (see below), but seeds can also be sown in 7.5cm/3in-wide pots during mid-spring and placed in 18°C/64°F. After germination, lower the temperature and gradually acclimatize plants to outdoor conditions. Plant outdoors when all risk of frost has passed.

COURGETTES
These are like small marrows and are usually harvested when only 10cm/4in long. They are grown in the same way as marrows, but the range of varieties is different. Because they are bush varieties they do not need to be 'stopped'. Varieties include:
• 'Blondy': A hybrid with creamy-green, very sweet fruits.
• 'Gold Rush': Very prolific, with yellow fruits.
• 'Golden Zucchini': Excellently flavoured, creamy flesh.
• 'Zucchini': Prolific, with dark green fruits. Widely grown.

VARIETIES

These can be used fresh in summer or stored for winter.
• *'Early Gem': A hybrid, producing early fruits.*
• *'Green Bush': Can be cut when small as courgettes, or left until late summer to produce marrows.*
• *'Long Green Striped': Very prolific fruiting.*
• *'Long Green Trailing': Large fruits; frequently used by exhibitors.*

1. PREPARE *the planting positions in late spring. Choose a warm, sheltered site and dig out a hole 30cm/12in deep and 38cm/15in across. Fill the hole, forming a mound with a mixture of topsoil and decayed garden compost.*

2. IN LATE SPRING – *or early summer in cold areas – sow three seeds 18mm/¾in deep and about 7.5cm/3in apart. Placing a jam jar over the seeds hastens germination. When the young plants are 5cm/2in high, thin to the strongest.*

3. KEEP *the soil moist and pinch out the growing tips on lateral shoots on trailing varieties when 45–60cm/ 1½–2ft long. Bush types do not need 'stopping'. Cut the fruits when young to encourage the growth of further fruit.*

ONIONS
❖

 ONIONS are easily grown and introduce rich flavours to salads and cooked dishes. There are two main types of onion:

• 'bulbing' types are mainly sown in spring for harvesting during late summer and autumn of the same year. It is also possible to sow hardy varieties, such as 'Reliance' and 'Autumn Queen', in late summer, to produce onions during early and mid-summer of the following year. This is rather a rarity and the information here is for spring-sown types.

• 'spring' onions are delicious in salads and are detailed on the opposite page.

Spring onions are detailed on the opposite page.

VARIETIES

Bulbing onions
These are the onions that are grown for their large, rounded bulbs. Spring onions are detailed on the opposite page.
• *'Ailsa Craig': Well-known, with large, globe-shaped bulbs. But they do not store very well.*
• *'Bedfordshire Champion': Large, globular bulbs that store quite well.*
• *'Buffalo': A hybrid with early bulbs, but they do not store well.*
• *'Noordhollandse Bloedrode': Attractive red-skinned bulbs that can be stored for a long time.*
• *'Rijnsburger': Large, globular, straw-coloured bulbs that are excellent for storing.*

HARVESTING AND USING
Part of the skill in growing bulbing onions is harvesting and ripening them. Unless care is taken about this task the bulbs have a limited storage time. Towards the end of summer – and if the leaves have not naturally toppled over – bend over the stem just above the bulb to prevent growth being directed to the leaves. A few weeks later, use a garden fork to break the roots. The bulbs can then be laid on the soil's surface to ripen.

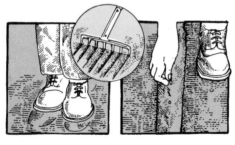

1. IN PREPARATION *for sowing seeds in spring, dig the ground in early winter and add plenty of garden compost or manure. In late winter, check the soil is slightly alkaline (see pages 12 and 13). Tread the soil firm and rake level.*

2. DURING *early spring, use a draw hoe to form drills 12mm/½in deep and 23cm/9in apart. If the soil is dry, water it a few days before sowing seeds. Sow seeds thinly and evenly; carefully cover and firm friable soil over them.*

3. SEEDS *germinate within three weeks and when the seedlings have straightened up and are about 5cm/2in high they must be thinned. First, ensure the soil is moist, then thin them 5cm/2in apart. Then trim them again later to 10cm/4in.*

Preferably, the base of each bulb should face the sun. Turn the bulbs regularly to ensure they are evenly ripened. When they are dry, store them on trays in a dry, vermin-proof, well-aerated shed. Alternatively, tie them into onion ropes or put in net bags.

If the weather is wet, the bulbs will have to be ripened on sacking in a shed or a greenhouse. Another way is to place them in a cold frame or under cloches.

ONION SETS

Bulbing onions are sometimes grown from 'onion sets'. These are small, partly-developed onion bulbs which have been stored during winter. They are especially useful in cold regions, where the growing season is short.

Plant sets in the latter part of early spring and into mid-spring. Prepare the soil in the same way as for sowing seed. Mark out rows 25cm/10in apart and push the sets into the ground so that just the top can be seen. Space the sets about 10cm/4in apart and thoroughly water the soil. Cover with hoops of wire netting.

SPRING ONIONS

Spring onions, also known as salad onions, bunching onions and scallions, are ideal for pulling and using in salads. Sometimes, the thinnings from bulbing onions are used in salads, but there are special varieties of spring onions, including 'White Lisbon' and 'Ishikura'.

Prepare the soil in the same way as for bulbing onions and sow seeds 12mm/½in deep in drills 10–13cm/4–5in apart every two weeks from early spring to the early part of mid-summer. This produces spring onions from early summer to early autumn. Water the soil before pulling up spring onions.

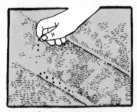

Sowing seeds thinly

4. WATER THE SOIL *during dry periods and carefully hoe around the bulbs to remove weeds. By late summer or early autumn, encourage bulbs to ripen by sharply bending over the foliage immediately above each bulb's neck.*

5. A FEW WEEKS *later, use a garden fork to prise under the bulbs to break their roots and thereby stop them growing. Take care not to bruise the bulbs as this will reduce their storage ability and immediately encourage the onset of decay.*

6. A FEW DAYS *after forking under the bulbs, lift them completely, carefully rub off soil and place them on the surface to dry and ripen further. If the weather is wet they will have to be dried on sacking in a well-ventilated shed or greenhouse.*

PEAS

❖

 DRIED peas have been used in cooking for many centuries, but growing peas for eating fresh started only a few hundred years ago. By sowing seeds in the open, from early spring to early summer, it is possible to harvest fresh peas from early to late summer. And by making a sowing of a variety of 'first-early' peas (such as 'Kelvedon Wonder') it is possible to extend harvesting until autumn.

SOIL PREPARATION AND SOWING

Prepare the soil in the way suggested below. When sowing seeds there are two main choices: either in flat-bottomed drills, where the seeds can be sown in three rows with about 7.5cm/3in between them, or in two V-shaped drills 20cm/8in apart. Germination takes about seven to ten days. Whichever method is used, a wide row of young pea plants is produced. The distance between the rows is dictated by the height of the variety (see right).

VARIETIES

Garden peas are classified into three groups according to the time they are harvested.

First early peas
From sowing to harvesting takes about twelve weeks.
- *'Hurst Beagle': 45cm/1½ft. Sweet and juicy.*
- *'Kelvedon Wonder': 45cm/1½ft high. Versatile variety.*
- *'Little Marvel': 45cm/1½ft high. Good flavour.*

Second early peas
From sowing to harvesting takes thirteen to fourteen weeks.
- *'Hurst Green Shaft': 75cm/2½ft high. Heavy cropping.*
- *'Onward': 75cm/2½ft high. Heavy crops of plump peas.*

Main-crop peas
From sowing to harvesting takes fourteen to sixteen weeks.
- *'Lord Chancellor': 1m/3½ft high. Heavy crops of superb peas.*
- *'Senator': 75cm/2½ft high.*
- *'Trio': 75cm/2½ft high.*

1. IN EARLY WINTER, *dig the soil and add garden compost or manure. Test if the soil is acid; dust the surface with lime in late winter if acid. Form a flat-bottomed trench, 25cm/10in wide and 6cm/2½in deep.*

2. SOW SEEDS *7.5cm/3in apart in three staggered rows in the base of the flat-bottomed trench. Alternatively, use a draw hoe to take out a pair of V-shaped drills, 6cm/2½in deep and 20cm/8in apart.*

3. IF MORE *than one row is being grown, space them to the expected height of the variety being sown, usually 45–90cm/1½–3ft. Birds soon devastate rows of newly sown seeds; place hoops of wire netting over the rows.*

4. INSERTING *pea sticks into the ground on either side of a row of peas is the traditional way to support plants. Put the sticks in early, so that plants grow up and through the twigs, eventually covering them.*

5. AN ALTERNATIVE *method of supporting plants is to use wide-meshed wire netting, 90cm – 1.2m/ 3–4ft high. Erect the netting when the plants are 5cm/ 2in high and use stout poles or canes to hold it upright.*

6. FROM *the latter part of early summer to autumn, pick the pods when young and tender. Regularly harvesting the pods encourages more pods to develop. Those at the base are ready first.*

KEYS TO SUCCESS

Garden peas are not the easiest crop to grow as they are vulnerable to pests such as birds and the notorious pea moth, which enters peas and makes them inedible. Nevertheless, with care a good crop can be grown. Here are a few hints for producing a successful crop of peas:

• Never sow seeds in cold, wet soil. Either choose a well-drained site or wait a few weeks until spring or early summer sun has dried and warmed up the soil.

• Always choose fertile soil. Add garden compost or manure when preparing the soil in early winter.

• Ensure the soil is not acid. Test the soil in late winter (see pages 12 and 13).

• Choose the right variety for the time of year (see opposite page).

• Protect seeds from birds by covering the rows with netting.

• Water plants if there are dry periods.

• Spray the plants with insecticides every ten days after the start of flowering.

ASPARAGUS PEAS

ASPARAGUS PEAS, *often known as winged peas, develop pods about 36mm/ 1½in long that are cooked and eaten whole. If left to grow long, they become tough and inedible. Sow seeds in late spring (early summer in cold areas), in drills 2.5cm/ 1in deep and 30cm 12in apart. Space the seeds 10–15cm/ 4–6in apart. Keep the plants well watered once the flowers have formed; if heavily watered initially the yield is diminished.*

Support the plants when young by using twiggy sticks. Pick the pods regularly while they are young.

POTATOES

❖

POTATOES are native to South America and when found by Spaniards were said to resemble 'floury truffles'. They were soon introduced to Europe and have become a main part of many diets. They are easily grown but must not be planted too early in cold areas as frost soon kills young stems and leaves. In autumn their growth is curtailed by frost.

IN CONTAINERS

Tubs on patios make splendid novelty homes for potatoes. Plant second-early varieties on a few inches of compost in a tub and cover with 13cm/5in of friable soil or compost, adding more as the stems grow. Growing-bags are other suitable containers.

PREPARING THE 'SEEDS'

The 'seeds' are small, healthy potatoes retained from the previous year's crop. These are best bought from reputable seed companies who sell virus-free stock.

They are usually bought in late winter and must be placed in clean boxes containing about 2.5cm/1in of dry peat. Space out the 'seeds', with the rose end (sprouting end) uppermost. Put them in a light, airy place such as a cool but frost-proof greenhouse or shed.

Within five to six weeks, sturdy shoots 18–25mm/³⁄₄–1in long will have formed. Leave these shoots

intact, taking care not to knock them off when planting. This process of encouraging shoots to form is known as 'chitting'. It is essential for early varieties, and beneficial for main-crop types. Chitting potatoes encourages rapid growth.

PREPARING THE SOIL

Dig the soil in late summer, but do not add manure. Neither apply lime in late winter but dust the surface and rake in a general fertilizer a couple of weeks before planting is to be carried out.

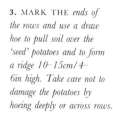

1. IN EARLY *and mid-spring, use a spade or draw hoe to form 15cm/6in deep drills. For early varieties, space the rows 60cm/2ft apart, but for main-crop types make the spacings wider at 75cm/2½ft.*

2. PLANT *'seed' potatoes in the bases of the V-drills. Space the 'seeds' of early varieties 30cm/12in apart; put main-crop types 38cm/15in apart. Position the buds (eyes) so that they face upwards.*

3. MARK THE *ends of the rows and use a draw hoe to pull soil over the 'seed' potatoes and to form a ridge 10–15cm/4–6in high. Take care not to damage the potatoes by hoeing deeply or across rows.*

VARIETIES

Potato varieties are classified according to the time they can be planted.

First-early potatoes
These are the first varieties to be ready for harvesting. The 'seed' potatoes are planted in early spring (a few weeks later in cold areas) and tubers harvested in early and mid-summer.

- 'Arran Pilot': Heavy cropping, but not suitable for cold areas.
- 'Duke of York': Succeeds in most areas and soil.
- 'Epicure': Ideal in cold areas.
- 'Sutton's Foremost': High yield and good flavour.

Second-early potatoes
These are planted in mid-spring and harvested in mid to late summer.

- 'Estima': Heavy cropping.
- 'Great Scot': Heavy crops and stores well. Ideal for baking.
- 'Wilja': High, reliable yields. Good flavour.

Main-crop potatoes
These are planted in the latter part of mid-spring and harvested in early and mid-autumn. It is also possible to lift some in late summer for immediate use.

- 'Desiree': Good flavour and resistant to drought.
- 'Majestic': An old variety; ideal for making chips.

HARVESTING

This is also known as 'lifting' and must be tackled with care to avoid damaging the potatoes. Do not lift early varieties before the flowers are fully open. Then, use a trowel to remove soil and to check if the tubers are about the size of a hen's egg. If possible, use a potato fork to lift them. To harvest main-crop varieties, cut off the leaves and stems once they have withered and turned brown. Clear this away and a week later dig up the tubers. Allow the tubers to dry on the soil's surface for a few hours, then place in boxes and store in a dark, frost-free shed.

4. THROUGHOUT *summer, water the soil and regularly draw up soil around the shoots. Do not completely cover the leaves. Eventually, the ridges will be 30–38cm/12–15in high. Earthing-up helps kill weeds.*

5. EARLY *varieties can be dug up during early and mid-summer. Use a potato fork (it has wide, flat tines) to carefully dig up the potatoes. Main-crop varieties are harvested from late summer onwards.*

6. REMOVE *all soil and store the tubers in boxes in a frost-free, dry, vermin-proof shed. Regularly inspect the tubers and remove those showing signs of decay. If left, the rot spreads to all the other potatoes.*

PARSNIPS

 DIG soil in early winter but do not add manure or garden compost. Neither add lime in late winter, but a couple of weeks before sowing, rake in a general fertilizer. Stony soil and fresh manure soon distort and split parsnip roots.

EXHIBITION PARSNIPS

Growing exhibition parsnips is not difficult. Dig the soil deeply in early winter; do not add manure or compost. In spring, use a crow-bar to form holes about 90cm/3ft deep. Fill these with potting soil and sow seeds of an exhibition variety in the normal way.

Throughout summer, keep the soil moist to prevent roots crack-ing. Lift them only slightly prior to the exhibition day. Cut off any rootlets, wash off soil and wrap the roots in damp cloth to reduce the chance of them cracking.

HARVESTING

Some varieties mature early, but most parsnips are left until the foliage begins to die down in autumn. Frost soon causes the foliage to brown and die. Indeed, it is often claimed that the roots are sweeter and better after the onset of frost in autumn or winter.

VARIETIES

- *'Avonresister': Ideal in small gardens, as it takes less space than normal types. Sow spaced clusters of seeds every 7.5cm/3in, not the normal 15cm/6in.*
- *'Gladiator': A hybrid variety that is resistant to canker and is very early maturing.*
- *'Hollow Crown Improved': Long roots and often used for exhibition, as well as in kitchens.*
- *'Offenham': Broad-shouldered variety and ideal for growing on shallow soils.*
- *'Tender and True': Very long roots, resistant to canker and revealing a good flavour.*

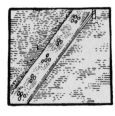

1. IN EARLY SPRING *sow three seeds (about 2.5cm/1in apart) in clusters 15cm/6in apart in drills 12–18mm/ ½–¾in deep. Space the drills 30cm/12in apart if more than one row of parsnips is being grown.*

2. KEEP *the soil moist and when the seedlings have germinated and produced several leaves, thin each cluster to the strongest and healthiest seedling. Re-firm the soil by gently watering the plants.*

3. HOE BETWEEN *the rows, taking care not to damage the plants. Water the soil regularly, especially during dry periods. From autumn onwards, use a garden fork to dig up and to lift the roots.*

RADISHES

❖

RADISHES are ideal in salads, but varieties with roots 30cm/12in or more long have been introduced, and these can be cooked. Summer radishes are the most popular, while early crops can be grown by using cloches (see below). Also, there are winter types (right).

WINTER RADISHES

These are sown in the same way as summer types, but the rows spaced 23cm/9in apart. Thin the seedlings to about 15cm/6in apart. Re-firm soil around the roots and keep the ground moist. During late autumn, lift the roots. Store them in boxes of dry sand.

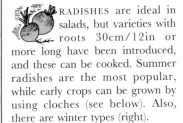

EARLY RADISHES

Dig the soil in autumn, and in early winter break down the surface with a rake and place low cloches in a row over the soil. Placing the cloches over soil, in advance of sowing, helps it to warm up and to encourage rapid germination. Sow seeds in mid or late winter, 12mm/½in deep in rows 10cm/4in apart. Thin the seedlings to 2.5cm/1in apart. Use a quick-maturing variety such as the popular 'Scarlet Globe' with round, bright red roots.

VARIETIES

Summer radishes
• 'April Cross': Roots 30–38cm/12–15in long.
• 'Cherry Belle': Globular.
• 'French Breakfast': Oblong.
• 'Juliette': Globular.
• 'Pontvil': Oblong.
• 'Prinz Rotin': Globular.
• 'Red Prince': Globular.
• 'Scarlet Globe': Globular.

Winter radishes
• 'Black Spanish Round': Large and globular.
• 'Black Spanish Long': Roots up to 30cm/12in long.
• 'Mino Early': Long roots, up to 30cm/12in long, and with a mild flavour.

1. FROM *mid-spring to late summer, sow seeds every two weeks. Form drills 12mm/½in deep and 15cm/6in apart. Do not space the rows any closer, as it is then difficult to step between them.*

2. IT IS *essential to sow seeds evenly and thinly along the rows. Cover the seeds and firm friable soil over them. Sowing seeds thickly is a waste of seed and can result in congested seedlings that encourage diseases.*

3. GERMINATION *takes between five and seven days and when the seedlings are established and large enough to handle, thin them to 2.5cm/1in apart. Re-settle the soil around the roots by watering it.*

SHALLOTS

❖

SHALLOTS have a milder flavour than onions and therefore are often more popular. They are planted in late winter and by the latter part of mid-summer a single bulb will have produced a cluster of eight to twelve bulbs (often known as daughter bulbs). From a row 3m/10ft long of newly planted shallot bulbs, expect to harvest about 3kg/7lb of new bulbs. They are easily grown and for gardeners new to vegetable growing can be a very satisfying crop to grow. The bulbs remain in good condition for a long time after harvesting.

VARIETIES

- *'Dutch Yellow'*: Popular, widely grown and frequently used in the kitchen.
- *'Golden Gourmet'*: Large crops of bulbs that store well.
- *'Hative de Niort'*: Deep-brown skin and widely grown by exhibitors. Well-shaped bulbs, but few in number.

GARLIC

This bulbous-rooted plant is better known in Continental cookery than in Britain. It has a strong flavour and bouquet and must be used sparingly. Well-drained soil and a sunny position are essential. In late winter, buy a few garlic bulbs from a greengrocer and split them into cloves (segments). Plant them 2.5cm/1in deep – and with their pointed-end uppermost – 10cm/4in apart in rows with 20cm/8in between them. Looking after them is easy; just remove weeds and keep the soil moist during dry periods. In late summer the leaves turn yellow and bend over. Use a garden fork to loosen soil under them and place the bulbs on the surface to dry and ripen. Store them in a frost-free and airy shed.

1. DIG SOIL *in early winter and add well-decayed manure or compost. In mid-winter, check that the soil is not acid. In late winter, push shallot bulbs into the soil, 15cm/6in apart in rows 20cm/8in apart.*

2. LEAVE *each bulb's top slightly above the surface and cover with a hoop of wire netting as protection against birds. Use an onion hoe to remove weeds and in mid-summer scrape soil from around each bulb.*

3. FROM *mid-summer onwards, as soon as the leaves become yellow, use a garden fork to dig up clusters of bulbs. Brush off the soil and separate them into individual bulbs. Store in a cool, dry, airy shed.*

SPINACH

❖

Spinach has its admirers and is acclaimed when combined with poached eggs. Fertile, moisture-retentive soil and regular watering are essential for this crop. In early winter, dig the soil and add plenty of well-rotted garden compost or manure. Dust the soil with lime in late winter, if it is acid, and rake in a general fertilizer a couple of weeks before sowing the seeds.

VARIETIES

Summer spinach
• *'King of Denmark': An old variety, with leaves borne well above soil level and therefore do not readily become splashed by rain first falling on soil.*
• *'Long-standing Round': Ideal for early sowings.*
• *'Norvak': Relatively new. Prolific crops and ideal for sowing in mid-summer.*
• *'Sigmaleaf': Long cropping, and can also be used as a winter variety.*

WINTER SPINACH

By sowing seeds in late summer and early autumn it is possible to produce spinach for harvesting from mid-autumn to mid-spring.

Choose a sunny site, with well-drained but moisture-retentive soil. The soil should have been dug during the previous early winter and garden compost or manure added. In late summer, lightly fork the soil, rake level and sow seeds 18mm/³⁄₄in deep in

drills 38cm/ 15in apart. After germination, first thin the seedlings to 7.5cm/3in apart, later 15cm/6in. Harvest the leaves when ready and from mid-autumn cover with cloches.

Varieties to choose include 'Monnopa' (good flavour), 'Sigmaleaf' (see summer varieties) and 'Broad-leaved Prickly' (dark green and fleshy leaves). In addition, the plants do not readily run to seed (bolt).

1. SOW SEEDS *every two weeks from early spring to mid-summer. Form drills 12–18mm/½– ¾in deep and 30cm/12in apart. Draw soil over the drills and firm it. Gently but thoroughly water the soil.*

2. KEEP *the soil moist. Germination takes up to three weeks and when the seedlings are established, thin them to 7.5cm/3in apart. Later, when the leaves touch, thin them to 15cm/6in apart.*

3. FROM *sowing to maturing takes up to thirteen weeks (slightly less for sowings in early and mid-summer). Harvest the leaves as soon as they are a reasonable size, starting with the outer ones.*

TOMATOES

 OUTDOOR tomatoes are very quickly killed by frost and therefore cannot be planted outside until late spring or early summer, when the risk of cold nights has passed. Prepare the soil in early winter by digging in plenty of well-decayed garden compost or manure. In late winter, dust the soil with lime if it is acid (see pages 12 and 13).

PLANTS AND PLANTING

Plants are raised from seeds sown in 13°C/55°F in a greenhouse, but if only a few plants are needed it is better to buy them. Choose sturdy plants, about 20cm/8in high and with dark green leaves. Do not buy thin and lanky plants, with long spaces between the leaf joints. These will never recover and become strong.

When planting, ensure that the top of the root-ball is only fractionally below the surface of the soil. Water the soil thoroughly after planting and use slug pellets to protect the plants, which are soon damaged by slugs.

VARIETIES

There is a wide range of tomato varieties to grow outdoors. Most are grown as cordons (upright and supported by a cane) while some are bush types, usually no more than 75cm/2½ft high, but sometimes less.

Cordon tomatoes
- *'Alicante'*: 60cm/2ft apart.
- *'Moneymaker'*: 75cm/2½ft apart.
- *'Outdoor Girl'*: 60cm/2ft apart.
- *'Sweet 100'*: 75cm/2½ft apart. Masses of cherry-sized fruits.

Bush tomatoes
- *'Florida Petit'*: 23–30cm/ 9–12in apart. Ideal for windowboxes.
- *'Pixie'*: 45cm/1½ft apart.
- *'Red Alert'*: 45cm/1½ft apart.
- *'Sub-arctic Plenty'*: 45cm/ 1½ft apart. Early cropping. It is ideal for cool areas.
- *'Tiny Tim'*: 30–80cm/12–15in.

1. WHEN *all risk of frost has passed, knock in 1.5–1.8m/5–6ft-long posts, spacing them 45cm/1½ft apart with 75–90cm/2½–3ft between them. Position a plant on the sunny side of each cane.*

2. TAKE *care not to damage the stem when setting a plant in position. Make sure that the top of the soil-ball is fractionally below the surface. Tie the stem to the cane, taking care to allow for subsequent growth.*

3. CONTINUE *to tie the stem to a supporting cane or pole, and remove shoots that develop from the leaf joints. Bend them sideways until they snap off. However, do not remove those growing on bush varieties.*

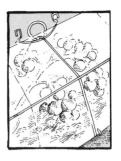

4. WHEN *a plant has formed four trusses (a flower stem which later will bear fruits) snap off the leading shoot just above the second leaf truss. Outdoor plants will not normally produce and ripen more than four trusses.*

5. PICK *the fruits when ripe. While picking them, do not squeeze. Instead, hold them in the palm of your hand and snap off the stem so that the calyx (the green, star-like growth) is attached to the fruit.*

6. IN EARLY AUTUMN *cut the tomato plants from their supports and lay them in a line on a bed of straw. Tall cloches can then be placed over them and the fruits left to ripen. Water the soil, but do not dampen the fruits.*

TOMATOES ON A PATIO

Warm, wind-sheltered patios are ideal homes for tomatoes, whether in growing-bags, pots, windowboxes or hanging baskets. It is essential, however, to select the right variety for each place. Some varieties are 'cordon' types, and therefore need to have sideshoots removed; 'bush' types do not. When planting tomatoes in window boxes, choose varieties such as 'Tiny Tim' and 'Florida Petit'.

STANDARD *sized growing-bags create ideal homes for two cordon-type plants. Ensure the compost remains evenly moist and use proprietary wire frames to support the plants.*

TOMATOES IN HANGING BASKETS

Hanging baskets are unusual places for tomato plants. It is essential to choose suitable varieties and to ensure that the compost does not become dry. The variety 'Tumbler' is ideal, with sweetly-flavoured, bright red, cherry-like fruits. Do not put the plants outside until all risk of frost has passed, and select a warm, sunny and wind-sheltered position. Use a large hanging basket and line it with a thick layer of sphagnum moss to help retain moisture in the compost.

SWEETCORN

❖

SWEETCORN must be grown in blocks, rather than in single lines, to assist with pollination. Seeds can be sown where they will grow or, for early crops and especially in cool regions, plants can be raised in gentle warmth (see details below).

Prepare the soil in early winter by digging and adding decayed garden compost or manure. In late winter, apply lime if the soil is acid. Later, in mid-spring, dust the surface with a general fertilizer and rake it into the soil.

VARIETIES

- *'Earliking': Sweet and ideal for growing in cold areas.*
- *'Early Extra Sweet': Very sweet; do not mix it with other sweetcorn varieties.*
- *'John Innes Hybrid': Early and reliable.*
- *'Polar Vee': Early cropping and good in cold regions.*
- *'Tokay Sugar': Early, sweet and pure white.*

1. WHEN *the risk of frost has passed, sow three seeds 2.5cm/1in deep, in clusters and 38cm/15in apart in rows 45cm/1¼ft apart. This is usually in late spring, although in cold areas a little later.*

2. AFTER *germination and when the plants are established, remove the weakest seedlings to leave one plant in each position. Re-firm soil around them and in summer water plants during dry periods.*

3. IN LATE SUMMER, *harvest the heads when the silks (at the top of the cob) have withered and the grains, when pressed, exude a creamy liquid. Twist the cob downwards to remove it.*

RAISING EARLY PLANTS

In mid-spring, sow seeds in a greenhouse. Use 7.5cm/3in-wide peat pots (to avoid root disturbance later) and sow two seeds, 2.5cm/1in deep, in each pot. Water and place in gentle warmth (10–13°C/50–55°F). After germination, remove the weaker seedlings, reduce the temperature slightly and slowly acclimatize plants to outdoor conditions. Plant them outdoors only when all risk of frost has passed. An alternative method is to sow seeds outdoors and to cover them with cloches. Put the cloches in place about three weeks before sowing in late spring, so the soil can warm up.

TURNIPS

❖

TURNIPS are too frequently considered to be tough and woody vegetables eaten solely during winter. They are not; indeed, early sowings can be used in salads, while later crops are harvested in summer. Main-crop turnips are ready for lifting in autumn for eating in winter.

During early winter, dig the soil but do not add garden compost or manure. Do not add lime but a couple of weeks before sowing seeds in mid-spring, dust and rake in a general fertilizer.

VARIETIES

Early turnips
• *'Jersey Navet'*: Ideal for very early sowings under cloches.
• *'Snowball'*: Globular and quick-growing. Ideal for sowing under cloches.
• *'Tokyo Cross'*: Quick-maturing, with small, globe-like roots.

Main-crop turnips
• *'Golden Ball'*: Fleshy and tender roots that keep for a long time.

1. SOW EARLY *turnips from early spring to early summer to produce edible roots from late spring to late summer. Sow seeds 12–18mm/⅟₂–¾in deep in drills 23cm/9in apart. Use early varieties.*

2. EARLY *sowings are usually left unthinned and the plants pulled up and eaten raw in salads. If larger roots are wanted from these early sowings, thin the seedlings so that they are 13cm/5in apart.*

3. MAIN-CROP TURNIPS *are sown during mid-summer to produce roots for lifting during early and mid-autumn. Thin these to 23cm/9in apart: these are the ones for storing and use during winter.*

TURNIP TOPS AS GREENS

Turnips tops are a popular vegetable for harvesting in early and mid-spring. Choose a main-crop variety and sow seeds in early autumn, 12–18mm/⅟₂–¾in deep in drills only 10cm/4in apart.
By sowing seeds evenly and thinly the young seedlings do not need to be thinned. During early spring, when the tops are 10–15cm/4–6in high, harvest the leaves, but leave the roots to sprout again for a further crop. In mild areas, several crops can be cut from them.

PESTS AND DISEASES

❖

VEGETABLES soon become irreparably damaged by pests and diseases, perhaps destroying a whole season's work. Some problems can be prevented by dusting soil with insecticides before sowing or planting, or by treating the seeds. Once plants are attacked by insects, regular spraying is usually the only solution.

Some diseases are most active when plants, which are too close together, are wet; although garden space may be small, never put plants closer than the space recommended. Soil pests like wireworms and leatherjackets are most destructive on pasture land newly converted to a vegetable plot.

When selecting chemicals to control problems with vegetables, always read the instructions and check its suitability for that particular crop. Also, ensure that the time recommended between spraying and harvesting is strictly observed. Wash all vegetables before eating.

APHIDS, *also known as greenfly and blackfly, infest leaves and shoots, sucking sap and causing distortion. They also transmit viruses. Use an insecticide regularly throughout summer.*

ASPARAGUS BEETLES *(square orange markings on a black body) soon strip stems of leaves. Spray with derris as soon as they are seen. Picking off beetles also helps to control them.*

CABBAGE ROOTFLIES *soon kill young plants by tunnelling into roots. Infested plants grow slowly and have blue-tinged leaves. Use an insecticide before setting plants in position.*

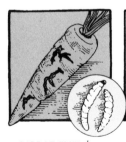

CARROT FLIES *have small, creamy maggots which devastate parsnips, celery and carrots. Rake in suitable insecticides before sowing seeds. As well, quickly remove and burn thinnings.*

CABBAGE CATERPILLARS *burrow into cabbages, devastating them. Pick them off by hand and regularly use insecticidal sprays. Inspect the undersides of leaves regularly for eggs.*

CELERY FLIES *have larvae which tunnel into leaves, causing them to shrivel and die. Spray with insecticides at the first sign of infestation. Also, pull off infected leaflets.*

CHOCOLATE SPOT *forms small, brown spots on the leaves of broad beans. Dig up and destroy infected plants and spray the remaining ones with a fungicide. Avoid soils rich in nitrogen.*

CLUB-ROOT *is a notorious disease of the cabbage family. Roots distort and plants die. Acid soil encourages the disease. Treat seedlings when they are being planted out with a suitable fungicide.*

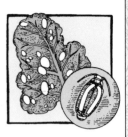

FLEA BEETLES *eat holes in the leaves of brassica seedlings, sometimes killing young plants, especially during dry seasons. Keep seedlings watered and treat seeds with an insecticide.*

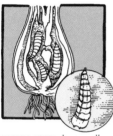

ONION FLIES *have small, white maggots that burrow into bulbs. Leaves turn yellow and wilt. Pull up and burn infected plants and rake insecticides into the soil before sowing or planting.*

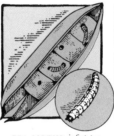

PEA MOTHS *infest pea pods and cause maggoty peas, making them unusable. Early and late crops sometimes escape attack. Use insecticides about seven days after the onset of flowering.*

PEA AND BEAN WEEVILS *chew notches from the edges of pea and broad bean plants. Regularly hoeing around plants helps to prevent attack; when first seen, use insecticides.*

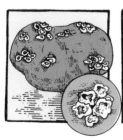

POTATO SCAB *creates raised, distorted, scabby areas on the skins of potatoes. Only the skin is affected, however; the tubers can still be cooked and eaten. Do not lime the soil.*

SLUGS AND SNAILS *soon destroy seedlings and soft-tissued plants. Pick off and destroy them and use baits along rows. Place under tiles and ensure dogs and cats cannot get at them.*

WIREWORMS *are soil pests that burrow into roots, bases of stems and tubers. The damage often encourages the entry of diseases, resulting in decay. Dust the soil with insecticides.*

VEGETABLE CALENDAR

❖

SPRING

Spring is a busy time in a vegetable garden.

- Prepare seed-beds in early spring in preparation for sowing seeds (14–15). Crops raised in this way include cabbages, cauliflowers, Brussels sprouts, asparagus, calabrese and leeks.
- Many vegetables are raised by sowing seeds outdoors in the positions where they will grow and mature (16–17).
- Hoe between young plants in spring to eradicate weeds and to create a fine tilth on the soil's surface (18–19).
- Water young plants to ensure rapid establishment (18–19).
- Plant suckers from established globe artichokes (20).
- Sow cardoons in spring (20).
- Plant tubers of Jerusalem artichokes in spring (21).
- Sow asparagus seeds in a seed-bed to raise new plants (22).
- Plant asparagus crowns (22).
- Sow broad beans (24).
- Sow French beans in late spring or early summer (25).
- In early spring, prepare the positions for runner beans (26).
- In late spring (in warm areas) sow runner beans (26).
- Sow beetroot seeds (28).
- Sow broccoli and calabrese (29).
- Sow Brussels sprouts seeds in a seed-bed (30).
- Plant Brussels sprouts (30).
- Harvest spring cabbages (32).
- Sow seeds of summer cabbage in seed-beds (32).
- Sow seeds of cauliflowers in mid to late spring (34).
- Sow carrots (36).
- Prepare celery trenches (38).
- Sow seeds of leeks (42).
- Sow marrows in late spring on slight mounds (43).
- Plant onion sets (44).

SUMMER

Looking after vegetables in summer ensures good crops.

- Hoe between young plants in spring to eradicate weeds and to create a fine tilth on the soil's surface (18–19).
- Water plants, especially during dry periods (18–19).
- Mulch plants in early summer, but first hoe off weeds and thoroughly water the soil (18–19).
- When applying weed-killers, use a dribble-bar (18–19).
- Protect newly sown seeds from birds by forming tunnels of wire netting (13–14).
- Install timing devices that control the time and period when water-sprinklers operate (18).
- Harvest asparagus spears early, when they are 13–15cm/5–6in high (23).
- Support broad beans in early summer (24).
- Pinch out the tops of broad bean plants when they are in full flower (24).
- Sow French beans in late spring or early summer (25).
- Harvest French beans from mid-summer onwards (25).
- In early summer (in cold areas) sow runner beans (26).
- Support runner beans (26–27).
- Pick runner beans regularly throughout summer (27).
- Use a sharp knife to harvest broccoli and calabrese (29).
- Draw up soil around the stems of Brussels sprouts (31).
- Foliar feed Brussels sprouts in mid-summer (31).
- Sow seeds of spring cabbage in mid to late summer (32).
- Plant summer cabbages in late spring or early summer (32).
- In summer, bend over leaves of cauliflowers to protect the curds from strong light (35).

AUTUMN

This is the time to harvest vegetables, especially those that are to be stored for use in winter. Choose a storage place that is cool but will not freeze, is dry and well aerated, and free from vermin.

Do not cram different vegetables together and ensure that they can be regularly inspected to ensure decay has not begun. Any that have developed rot must be removed immediately and all vegetables close to them inspected.

Vegetables that have been attacked by pests are more likely to become invested with storage rots than healthy ones.

Always label vegetables being put into store, so that they can be later judged for their keeping qualities and flavour. Many vegetables can be frozen; details of freezing some vegetables are given throughout this book.

After crops have been lifted in autumn, burn parts that are woody or have been infected with diseases or pests. And rake up all leaves and debris to prevent diseases and pests persisting until the following year.

- Harvest the tubers of Jerusalem artichokes (21).
- In late summer or early autumn, cut down asparagus stems to 7.5cm/3in above the soil (22–23).
- Harvest Brussels sprouts from autumn to late winter (30–31).
- Plant spring cabbage plants in early to mid-autumn (32).
- Harvest summer cabbages in late summer or early autumn (32).
- Harvest trench celery from late autumn to late winter (10).
- Dig up potatoes before the tubers are damaged by frost. Allow the potatoes to dry on the soil's surface before collecting and storing them (48–49).
- Harvest parsnips (50).

WINTER

Early winter is the time for preparing soil. Some crops require the addition of garden compost or well-decomposed manure, while others, such as beetroot, parsnips and carrots, do not. Check with the crop rotation chart on page 12 before digging the soil.

In late winter, test a soil sample to find out if it is acid or chalk. The chart on page 13 indicates the amount of lime required to correct acidity. Never add lime at the same time as incorporating manure into the soil.

Seed catalogues appear in early winter and orders for seeds need to be made to avoid disappointment during the following year. Seeds not used during the previous year can be sown during the following one, but invariably fewer will germinate, although keeping seeds for just one year is usually not a problem.

Digging the soil is a major task during early winter and most gardeners try to finish this job as soon as possible, so that frost, snow, rain and wind have an opportunity to break down and improve the soil by spring of the following year.

While digging, keep the spade's blade clean, especially in clay soil. Use a scraper or trowel to remove soil that adheres to it.

- In early winter, cut down globe artichokes and cover their bases with straw (20).
- Harvest Brussels sprouts from autumn to late winter (30–31).
- Harvest winter cabbages from early to late winter (10).
- Fold cauliflower leaves over the curds to protect them from frost and snow (35).
- Harvest cauliflowers (35).
- Harvest trench celery from late autumn to late winter (10).

GLOSSARY OF
VEGETABLE TERMS
❖

ACID: *Used to refer to soils with a pH below 7.0.*

AERATION: *Digging, forking and hoeing soil to encourage the entry of air.*

EARTHING-UP: *The practice of drawing up soil around plants to exclude light from them.*

ALKALINE: *Having a chalky nature and a pH above 7.0.*

BARE-ROOTED PLANT: *A plant lifted from the ground and with little soil around the roots. Although this term is usually used for deciduous shrubs when being transplanted in winter, it can also be applied to cabbages and other brassica plants. These are carefully lifted from a seed-bed and planted into their growing positions.*

BASE DRESSING: *An application of fertilizer just before sowing or planting. It is lightly raked into the surface soil.*

BLANCHING: *The exclusion of light from stems and shoots to whiten them.*

BOLTING: *The premature flowering and production of seeds. It is usually caused by a check to growth, such as on poor soils or through drought.*

CATCH CROP: *Sowing and growing quickly-maturing crops.*

CHARD: *The young stems of globe artichokes, salsify and seakale.*

CHITTING: *The germination or sprouting of seeds before they are sown. It is often applied to 'seed' potatoes.*

COMPOUND FERTILIZER: *One formed of the three main plant foods: nitrogen, phosphorus (phosphates) and potassium (potash).*

CROP ROTATION: *The yearly moving of a distinct type of crop from one area of a garden to another (see pages 12 and 13). When the same crop is grown in the same position year after year, it encourages the build-up of pests and diseases, and continually removes the same plant foods from the soil.*

CULTIVAR: *A relatively recent term for a variety that arises in cultivation.*

DIBBER: *A tool used to make a hole in the ground or compost into which seedlings or plants can be planted. Dibbers used to transfer seedlings are the thickness of pencils and about 15cm/6in long, while those used to plant cabbages are about 30cm/12in long and 5cm/2in in diameter.*

EARTHING-UP: *Drawing up soil with a draw hoe, or spade, to mound up soil around the bases of plants.*

EYE: *A bud; often used to describe the dormant buds on a potato tuber.*

F1 HYBRID: *Refers to a cross between two unrelated plants. Many new varieties of vegetables are now F1 types and have a uniform and often large and strong nature. Unlike an ordinary variety, the crop of an F1 type matures at about the same time.*

FOLIAR FEEDING: *Plant foods that are lightly sprayed on a plant's foliage. Plants react rapidly to this treatment.*

FRIABLE: *Fine, crumbly, relatively dry soil.*

FUNGICIDE: *A chemical used to prevent, control or eliminate a disease.*

GARDEN COMPOST: *Decayed vegetable kitchen waste such as cabbage leaves and potato peelings.*

GROWING SEASON: *The period during which plants can grow. It is dictated by the last frost of winter or spring, and the first one in autumn or early winter.*

HARDEN OFF: *Acclimatizing plants which have been raised in gentle warmth in a greenhouse to outdoor conditions. Plants are often hardened off by placing them in cold frames and removing the frames for a longer period each day.*

HAULM: *The aerial part of a vegetable crop and specifically used to refer to the stems and leaves of potato plants.*

HERBICIDE: *A chemical used to kill weeds.*

HUMUS: *Derived from the decomposition of organic material such as garden compost and manure.*

HYBRID: *A plant which is the result of a cross between two unrelated plants. They exhibit vigour and uniformity. Seed retained from F1 hybrids does not produce replicas of the parents.*

INSECTICIDE: *A chemical that kills insects.*

LEGUMES: *Vegetables such as peas and beans. These are well-known members of the Leguminosae family.*

LOAM: *Fertile, well-drained and good-quality topsoil.*

MULCH: *The creation of a layer of decayed organic material on the soil's surface. It prevents the growth of weeds and evaporation of moisture from the soil's surface. Also, it provides some food and keeps the soil cool in summer. Mulches can also be created from sheets of black plastic.*

MUTANT: *Another term for 'sport', which is the natural deviation of part of the plant from the normal. The flower colour may change, or parts may be bigger and better.*

NEUTRAL: *Used to refer to soil that is neither acid nor alkaline, with a pH between 6.5 and 7.0.*

OFFSETS: *Small bulbs which appear around or at the base of a mother bulb. This frequently happens to shallots.*

PAN: *A hard, often impervious layer beneath the soil's surface that prevents the drainage of water and growth of roots. It is essential that this layer is broken up by deeply digging the soil.*

pH: *A measure of the acidity or alkalinity of soil, assessed on a logarithmic scale which ranges from 0 to 14, with 7.0 as the chemically neutral figure. However, most plants grow best in soil with a pH of 6.5.*

PINCHING OUT: *Also known as stopping, it refers to the removal of a growing tip to encourage the production of sideshoots.*

PROTECTED CROPPING: *The use of cloches or garden frames to enable crops to be sown or planted earlier than normal, or to encourage the later maturing of plants or ripening of fruits.*

SEED LEAVES: *The first leaf or leaves developed by a germinating seed.*

SPIT: *The depth of a spade's blade; between 25cm/10in and 30cm/12in.*

SPORT: *see Mutant.*

SYSTEMIC FUNGICIDE: *A fungicide which permeates a plant's sap stream and is able to combat a disease at the earliest possible moment.*

SYSTEMIC INSECTICIDE: *An insecticide which enters a plant's sap stream, killing insects as soon as they suck the sap or chew the tissue.*

THINNING: *The removal of small seedlings to create more space for those that are left. Usually, thinning is carried out in two stages; first to half the desired distance, later to the full spacing.*

TILTH: *Fine, friable surface soil.*

TRANSPLANTING: *The moving of plants from a seed-bed to their growing positions.*

TRUE LEAVES: *Leaves which reflect the true nature of a plant's leaves.*

TRUSS: *A term used to describe a cluster of flowers or fruits.*

VARIETY: *A variation within a species that occurs naturally and not in cultivation.*

WEED: *A plant that is growing in the wrong place.*

WIND ROCK: *The buffeting or loosening of a plant's roots by wind on the foliage and stems.*

INDEX